# Music Education in Crisis

## THE BERNARR RAINBOW LECTURES
## AND OTHER ASSESSMENTS

Edited by Peter Dickinson

THE BOYDELL PRESS

ISBN  978 1 84383 880 7

The Boydell Press is an imprint of Boydell & Brewer Ltd
PO Box 9, Woodbridge, Suffolk IP12 3DF, UK
and of Boydell & Brewer Inc.
668 Mt Hope Avenue, Rochester, NY 14620-2731, USA
website: www.boydellandbrewer.com

A CIP catalogue record for this book is available from the British Library

The publisher has no responsibility for the continued existence or accuracy of URLs for external or third-party internet websites referred to in this book, and does not guarantee that any content on such websites is, or will remain, accurate or appropriate

Papers used by Boydell & Brewer Ltd are natural, recyclable products made from wood grown in sustainable forests

Designed and typeset in FF Scala Pro and Scala Pro Sans by David Roberts, Pershore, Worcestershire

Printed and bound in Great Britain by CPI Group (UK) Ltd, Croydon, CRO 4YY

# Contents

# Introduction and Acknowledgements

PETER DICKINSON

THE FIRST FIVE BERNARR RAINBOW LECTURES have been delivered over a period of twelve years. Each of the lectures conveys an individual message of relevance and distinction, and an awareness of what Bernarr Rainbow stood for in his life's work bound up with music education.[1] The publication of these lectures is an integral part of the ongoing Rainbow heritage, supported by the Bernarr Rainbow Trust, with further material to come.

Issues in the politics of education move so fast that there are inevitably references in all these lectures that rapidly became out of date. So we have invited John Stephens to provide a 2013 perspective to this collection. Things have changed – and usually not for the better. The arts in this country have lived through a golden age since World War II, although we may not always have appreciated it as such. However, the fundamental convictions expressed by all the lecturers are so important now and into the future that the Trust felt that the five Bernarr Rainbow Lectures, along with Sir Peter Maxwell Davies's lecture, should appear in more permanent form.

Baroness Warnock approached the subject of imagination as a philosopher, and, after establishing criteria, applied her findings to music. Today, with musical literacy either sidelined or regarded in some absurd way as élitist, it is salutary that she says 'a child who is not taught to read music is shut off from enormous areas of pleasure and understanding', and that 'the parallel between reading words and reading musical notation is quite close'. Bernarr Rainbow agreed: 'Theories that children should not be pestered to learn to spell, write grammatically or learn multiplication

---

1 Sir Peter Maxwell Davies wrote the foreword to the enlarged second edition, with Gordon Cox, of Rainbow's *Music in Educational Thought and Practice* (Woodbridge: Boydell Press, 2006).

tables later found a musical counterpart in arguments against teaching the use of notation'.[2]

In these days of the tyranny of the visual image, when no television documentary seems able to describe any event without a mock-up re-enactment, it is remarkable that Baroness Warnock extols the contribution that could still be made by radio. Anyone at, or close to, her generation can remember the influential BBC radio features for schools, where weekly programmes were used in classrooms to support or even substitute for a music teacher. In a context where DVD programmes are available for music teaching in schools without music specialists a comeback by radio seems unlikely. With young people so conditioned from birth by constant visual images it would be hard to maintain concentration.

Warnock also supports singing, saying that 'children suffer a serious deprivation if they do not have a teacher who can make singing, in class, a regular element in their education'. She goes on to cite rounds and canons as successful material. This gives cause for thought in these days when inherited musical repertoire of all kinds is too often subordinated to children doing their own thing. In 1985 Bernarr Rainbow agreed: 'Another casualty to current iconoclasm was class singing itself. Former high standards of school singing now earned scornful rejection as being artificially reminiscent of the cathedral chorister.'[3]

To finish, Warnock agreed that the canon of Western music is no longer the whole story – as is now abundantly clear – and she commended the role of a vigorous amateur musical culture.

Western classical music has suffered a severe setback in an era of mass democratic culture, but it is exactly that tradition which nourished Lord Moser in his early years in Berlin and which he is anxious to preserve. Oskar Adolf Hermann Schmitz called us 'das Land ohne Musik' in 1904, and Bernarr Rainbow used that title for his study *The Land without Music: Musical Education in England 1800–1860 and its Continental Antecedents*.[4]

---

2 Bernarr Rainbow, 'Onward from Butler: School Music, 1945–1885', in *Bernarr Rainbow on Music: Memoirs and Selected Writings*, ed. Peter Dickinson (Woodbridge: Boydell Press, 2010), p. 238.

3 Rainbow, 'Onward from Butler', p. 238.

4 See Nicholas Temperley's discussion, p. 153 below.

In 1992, at a conference on Finnish and British music, Erkki Toivanen said 'It is quite self-evident that music has not played a central role in defining English or British national identity – whatever that is.'[5] A broader perspective shows this is not true, as witnessed by the heritage of folk music, the continuous tradition of liturgical music and, in more popular fields, the international penetration of Gilbert and Sullivan, the Beatles, and Andrew Lloyd Webber – not to mention the most prominent individual composers such as Elgar, Delius, Vaughan Williams and Britten. British achievements in music since World War II have been outstanding and owe much to the BBC and the Arts Council. In both cases Moser rightly extols the arm's-length principle that has traditionally separated both these organisations from government control. It is of paramount importance that this distinction is maintained. From his wide range of experience with the leading arts organisations, Moser goes into considerable detail about where we should be heading. Some of this has been overtaken by events, but his overall message is clear and utterly convincing.

The third lecture was given by the late Professor John Paynter, a composer, an insider, and an international voice in the field of music education. He was concerned that children and young people should be able to make music as informally and creatively as they paint or draw – initially, at least, without the intervention of notation. Rainbow saw some dangers in applying creativity to the music lesson. He recognised the immediacy of bringing the techniques of *avant-garde* music into the classroom, as pioneered by George Self and Brian Denis, whom he appointed to his staff at the College of St Mark and St John, but he was reluctant to lose access to the standard repertoire of Western music linked to traditional skills such as singing and musical notation. However, Paynter influenced more than a generation of music teachers with his persuasive arguments for getting young people to produce their own music, and his legacy has been lasting.

John Stephens is another insider in the field of music education whose pioneering work in bringing professional performers into schools brought this kind of provision into the mainstream. He understands the

5 Erkki Toivanen, 'The Allure of Distant Strains: Musical Receptiveness of the Anglo-Saxon', in *Music and Nationalism in 20th-Century Great Britain and Finland*, ed. Tomi Mäkelä (Hamburg: Von Bockel Verlag, 1997), p. 56.

multi-faceted diversity of the whole scene and, on the basis of a wide and long experience, examines the mechanisms and personnel involved. He is thus eminently suited to writing a postlude to this collection and bringing the issues up to date in the second decade of the twenty-first century.

Gavin Henderson has already had a colourful and varied career. He understands the life of professional musicians from his own background, from managing orchestras and festivals, and as an influential principal of a conservatoire – initially Trinity College of Music (now Trinity Laban), where there was a strong music-education programme run by John Stephens. Henderson's work, which included directing the Dartington International Summer School, has convinced him of the impact music can have in the community based on the interaction of all age groups. Like the other speakers, he argues passionately for continued funding for the arts as a way of enhancing the lives of all involved.

So, of course, does Sir Peter Maxwell Davies; he supports John Paynter in insisting that 'there can be no real understanding of music without creating it'. He attacks the trivialisation of television, 'the opium of the people', which has become worse since he delivered his Royal Philharmonic Society lecture in 1995. With characteristic thrust, Davies similarly attacks the absurd notion that classical music is élitist: El Sistema, originating in Venezuela and widely imitated elsewhere, has disproved that. He also claims that this country has the finest performers and composers to be found anywhere. How fortunate we are to have a Master of the Queen's Music who is able to make the case in public so convincingly, and how essential it is for his warnings to be heeded. Serious music must not become extinct.

Rainbow's own contribution, included here, was written in 1994, towards the end of his life, for an Australian festschrift in honour of Sir Frank Callaway; it shows him looking back over a long career of involvements with music education. I have chosen to contrast Rainbow's views with those of John Paynter, who contributed to the same Australian symposium, and to include a statement there by Wilfrid Mellers, who was strongly committed to music education in the new music department he started at York University in 1964. His prophetic warnings about the shortcomings of 'our leaders' predict precisely the position we are in today. Some of the issues Rainbow raised, such as his unwavering support of tonic-sol-fa, have not gained ground; others have been rectified. But this is the way he saw the position at the time he was writing. The overall picture has changed in ways that Bernarr Rainbow could not have envisaged, but he would certainly have admired the stance taken by all these speakers from their different vantage points.

I have also included two contrasting reviews of *Bernarr Rainbow on Music*, to show the reception that Rainbow's work is receiving fifteen years after his death. These are reproduced by permission of *Music and Letters* and the *Journal of Historical Research in Music Education*.

In presenting these lectures, the Trust has been fortunate to collaborate with the Institute of Education, University of London; the Royal Society of Arts; the Guildhall School of Music; Trinity College of Music, now Trinity Laban; the Royal Over-Seas League; the Royal Philharmonic Society; and Sir Ian Wrigglesworth, then at UK Land Estates, who supported the receptions following the lectures.

I am grateful to all the contributors for permission to print their texts and, in some cases, for their adding a postscript. The Royal Philharmonic Society agreed to the publication of Sir Peter Maxwell Davies's lecture, and he allowed me to edit his text.

I appreciate the contributions from John Stephens, who has been ideally placed to bring matters up to date at the end of this first series of lectures, and from Gordon Cox, who read the typescript. I have also benefited over many years from the counsel of members of the Advisory Board – Sir Ian Wrigglesworth, Dr Gordon Cox, Professor George Odam, Dr Charles Plummeridge, John Stephens, and Professor Graham Welch. Since these Bernarr Rainbow Lectures go back to the founding of the Trust it is appropriate to acknowledge the contribution of earlier trustees, the Reverend Professor Anthony Kemp and Angela Richardson-Bunbury.

Finally, I have been very fortunate to work on another book with David Roberts as copy editor and designer. The staff at Boydell & Brewer, including Michael Middeke and Megan Milan, have loyally seen this project through.

Foxborough House, Aldeburgh, 2013

Bernarr Rainbow at Gipsy Hill College on retirement, 1977

# Bernarr Rainbow: A Biographical Note

F ROM THE LATER 1960s Bernarr Rainbow began to be recognised as
the leading authority on the history of music education. His 400-page
book *Music in Educational Thought and Practice* has been widely recognised
and used as a standard text in music education courses in many parts of
the world.[1]

Rainbow's writings are both practical and scholarly, as a list of titles
shows. He began with *Music in the Classroom* and *A Handbook for Music
Teachers*.[2] All Rainbow's subsequent books are now available from Boydell
and Brewer: *The Land without Music* (1967; repr. 1991); *The Choral
Revival in the Anglican Church, 1839–72* (1970; repr. 2001); *John Curwen:
A Critical Biography* (1980; repr. in *Bernarr Rainbow on Music*, 2010);
*Music and the English Public School* (1991, new enlarged edn. in progress);
*Four Centuries of Music Teaching Manuals, 1518–1932* (2009); and *Bernarr
Rainbow on Music: Memoirs and Selected Writings* (ed. Peter Dickinson, with
introductions by Gordon Cox and Charles Plummeridge, 2010). Rainbow
also edited a collection of primers on music teaching from originals in
various languages – the *Classic Texts in Music Education* – that is a major
landmark enhanced as further volumes become available.

Bernarr Joseph George Rainbow was born in Battersea, London, on
2 October 1914 and died at Esher on 17 March 1998. His grandfather
was a member of the Royal Household at Sandringham; his father was
a cabinet-maker at Buckingham Palace, and finally Curator of Pictures
at Hampton Court, where the family moved in 1931. Bernarr went to
Rutlish School, Merton, and held various posts as a church organist while
still a schoolboy. He then attended Trinity College of Music part-time

---

1 Bernarr Rainbow, *Music in Educational Thought and Practice* (Aberystwyth: Boethius
Press, 1989); 2nd edition enlarged with further chapters by Gordon Cox, a foreword
from Sir Peter Maxwell Davies, and a biographical introduction by Peter Dickinson
(Woodbridge: Boydell Press, 2006/paperback 2007).

2 *Music in the Classroom* (London: Heinemann, 1956; 2nd edn 1971); *A Handbook for
Music Teachers* (London: Novello, 1964; 2nd edn 1968).

while working in the map branch of HM Land Registry, Lincoln's Inn Fields.

The war interrupted his studies and he spent four years in the army serving in North Africa and Italy. Soon after his return he became Organist and Choirmaster of All Saints Parish Church, High Wycombe, and then the first music master to be appointed at the Royal Grammar School. He started the influential High Wycombe Festival in 1946 and, as conductor, performer and entrepreneur, affected the musical life of the entire region.

In 1952 Rainbow was appointed Director of Music at the Church of England teacher training establishment, the College of St Mark and St John, Chelsea. This brought him new opportunities, and it was here that he began his research. In addition to his music diplomas he gained three postgraduate degrees from the University of Leicester – the MEd (1964); PhD (1968); and that university's first DLit (1992). From 1973 to 1979 he was Head of the School of Music at Kingston Polytechnic (now University), and he founded the Curwen Institute in 1978. Rainbow was made an Honorary Fellow of Trinity College of Music in 1995 and in the following year he established the annual Bernarr Rainbow Award for school music teachers. This is now administered by the Institute of Education, University of London, under the auspices of the Bernarr Rainbow Trust – a registered charity that also supports other initiatives in music education such as the Bernarr Rainbow Lectures published here.

The Bernarr Rainbow Archive is at the Library of the Institute of Education; his family papers are at Hampton Court; and his collection of Christian and Jewish hymnals and other liturgical music is at the Maughan Library and Information Services Centre, King's College, London.

# PART I

# FIVE BERNARR
# RAINBOW LECTURES

*Inaugural Bernarr Rainbow Lecture,*
*given at the Institute of Education,*
*University of London, 6 October 1999*

# Music and the Imagination

## BARONESS WARNOCK

Mary Warnock, DBE, FBA, was created a Life Peer of Weeke in the City of Winchester in 1985. She was Mistress of Girton College, Cambridge, from 1985 to 1991, having previously studied at Oxford and held teaching posts and fellowships there. She has served on a remarkable number of committees representing major issues in society and politics. Her many influential books are on philosophy, education and social issues; at a recent count she had honorary degrees from sixteen universities.

IT IS A GREAT HONOUR to have been asked to inaugurate the Bernarr Rainbow Lectures and I am extremely grateful for the chance to honour a great teacher and a great historian of education, as well as a musician. I believe, as he did, in the central importance of music education, especially in school, and it is this that will be my theme this evening. Bernarr Rainbow would, I hope, have had some sympathy with this choice of topic. But, of course, his interests were much wider than this: he was a scholar in the history not merely of education but of the fascinating connections between music and the Church of England, a rich subject indeed, to which I hope another lecture in the series may soon be devoted. Speaking for a moment autobiographically, about my own musical education, indeed the education of my own imagination, I can say without hesitation that church music was central to it, and I often reflect sadly on the huge gap that exists in the education of most children, even intensely musical children, and even those who are educated at our specialist music schools such as the Purcell School, who never enter a cathedral, and who know nothing of the great body of English choral music. I shall say a little more about this later.

But first I must introduce the idea of imagination which is part of the title of my lecture this evening. It is difficult, when talking about psychological concepts such as that of imagination, to avoid dropping into a crude and compartmentalised language of faculties. If I do speak of imagination as a faculty, I must be understood to be speaking loosely. I do not wish to suggest that imagination is that with which you are enabled to do one specific sort of thing, while another sort of thing is done by perception, another by emotion and another by the intellect or reason. Although physiologists may tell us which part of the brain is most involved in these various kinds of mental activity, from experience we know that they are not wholly separate from one another. Reasoning, sensing, feeling, finding funny, imagining all occur together in the conscious thinking physical object which is a human being. With that warning, however, I will try to characterise the human imagination in its most general sense.

There is a remarkable passage at the end of his book *Speculum Mentis*, where the philosopher R. G. Collingwood writes as follows:

> A mind which knows its own changes is by that lifted above change. History – and the same is true of memory ... – is the mind's triumph over time. It is a commonplace of philosophy [beginning, I suppose he meant, with Plato], that whereas sensation is temporal, thought is eternal or extra-temporal: sensation apprehends the here and now, thought apprehends the everywhere and the always. Hence the abstract psychology which splits the mind up into a sensitive and an intellectual faculty paradoxically presents us with a picture of man as standing with one foot in time, the other in eternity. This is mythology, but it is true mythology.[1]

It is my view that it requires imagination to perform the trick of connecting the momentary and ephemeral with the permanent, the particular with the universal, and that it is imagination which allows man to stand with his feet so far astride. If we had no imagination, we would each of us be stuck firmly in the present. But each one of us is in fact conscious of ourselves as an individual – that is, as separate centres of experience and with lives of our own to lead; and this consciousness is connected essentially with our ability to think of our own past and, to a lesser extent, foresee our own future or plan it as we want it to be. Imagination thus allows us to conceive of ourselves as continuous beings, playing a part in a continuous and

1 R. G. Collingwood, *Speculum Mentis, or the Map of Knowledge* (Oxford: Clarendon Press, 1924), p. 301.

partly intelligible world with a past and a future, which we can roughly call the natural world.

But we do not exercise imagination only with regard to ourselves and our own self-image. Sartre defined imagination as the ability to think of what is not, and though this seems at first a rather pointless definition, in fact it is useful.[2] 'What is not' covers that which is in the past, that which is in the future, that which is absent, that which is possible rather than actual, that which is an abstraction rather than a particular concrete thing. There is one simple sense of 'imaginary' which refers to 'what is not' in the sense of 'what is not true', where we may think of the imaginary as standing in opposition to the real: an imaginary person being one who is not a living person but a fictional character; an imaginary illness as one which is derived from no virus or inherited gene, and which will never kill the person who suffers from it. We all know of children who have imaginary playmates who accompany them everywhere, but who are not part of the real world. In this sense of the word, novelists or playwrights may be thought to possess imagination in its strongest form.

> Such tricks hath strong imagination,
> That, if it would but apprehend some joy,
> It comprehends some bringer of that joy;
> Or in the night, imagining some fear,
> How easy is a bush supposed a bear![3]

This is a perfectly legitimate and intelligible sense of the word 'imagination'. But when Sartre speaks of the imaginary as concerned with 'what is not', he is thinking in much wider terms. In his sense, it requires imagination to envisage or contemplate anything which is other than that which is present to our senses at this moment. In this sense, scientific discovery, technological invention, the telling of stories, the reconstructions of history, the understanding of people other than ourselves, the setting up of moral ideals, the pursuit of religious or aesthetic visions are all functions of the imagination.

2 Jean-Paul Sartre, *The Psychology of the Imagination* (London: Methuen, 1972).

3 William Shakespeare, *A Midsummer Night's Dream*, act 5, scene 1.

There is undoubtedly a strong connection between the possession of imagination in this wide sense and the possession of language. For language is always pointing outwards, away from the here and now, to things which occur and recur – to a cat, for example, who is one of a kind of animals, not all of which are present, and perhaps to an individual of this kind who was around yesterday and who is probably now hiding, invisible, under the bushes. Through language we are able to refer to that which is not before our immediate eyes, and to refer to it in a way that other people than ourselves can understand. Indeed language points outwards also insofar as its use assumes the existence of other people than the person now speaking. It is essentially a device for communication – that is, communication with others. So, if one teaches a chimpanzee to speak words one might congratulate oneself on teaching it to use language, but it is not until the chimpanzee can say of its mother 'She wants a drink' that we begin to realise that this chimpanzee has acquired imagination. He is communicating not just about his own needs and sensations, but about those of others, not himself. He can think not only of his own thirst, the here and now, but about his mother's imagined thirst which is not his own.

However, though the connection is strong between the possession of imagination and the use of language, I shall argue that it is preferable to speak of imagination as concerned with meaning or significance rather than with language, though obviously these are connected too. But there is an important difference. In using language we are always trying to make things exact. Even the most inept language-users, those who have the most frequent recourse to expressions such as 'you know' or 'you know what I mean', may be seen to be struggling, through the medium of words, to convey with precision what they mean. And at the other end of the spectrum, refined users of language may write and rewrite a passage time and again to find the words, and indeed the syntax, which most closely express the nuances of what they wish to communicate. To succeed in this enterprise is of course a most important part of the function of imagination. And such language-users are essentially concerned with the meaning or significance of their words.

But besides this, there is another concept of significance with which imagination is bound up. This is the area where the significant is identical with the valuable. When Macbeth speaks of life as 'a tale told by an idiot, full of sound and fury, signifying nothing', we understand what he means:[4] a life in which nothing is held valuable, nothing worth pursuing, is a life that has no significance. It seems to me sadly true that there are many children at school for whom there is no significance in the lives they lead. What happens to them, whether at home or at school, is meaningless and without any value. We are frequently told that it is the duty of teachers to inculcate an understanding of values in their pupils, that this responsibility lies increasingly with them, as there is an erosion of values in society as a whole, and thus in the backgrounds of the children they teach. This duty to inculcate values is generally thought of as a matter of the teaching, as it is nowadays inelegantly expressed, of 'right from wrong'. And many teachers understandably wonder how they are supposed to do this, and why it should fall to them almost exclusively to do it. But one must remember that there are many other values besides those of morality. And it seems to me that it is with values other than the moral that a teacher's first duty must lie. I do not deny the duty of a school as a community to cause children to learn moral values and to live by them; but each individual teacher may have a duty that lies nearer the heart of his or her particular expertise. For one of the greatest obstacles to education, and, more important, one of the most depressing experiences of adolescence, is boredom. I suppose that this has always been so; but it seems a truism to say that boredom is more of a threat at the present time than it has been in the past, simply because of the materialistic nature of most children's aspirations. School children seem above all things to want possessions, and possessions of a particular kind: a special kind of training shoes, a particular make of watch, or whatever it may be. Numbers of them have almost unending access to television, of course, and more to computer games or the Internet. There seems nothing else for them to do except accumulate objects or sit in front of the screen. When these things are not possible, when they are actually in the classroom, they suffer agonies of boredom. Nothing seems of any value, what is presented to them is a 'tale told by an idiot'. It is thus, in my opinion the teacher's task to break through this deadening shroud of boredom and awake an interest which, even if not permanent, will nevertheless, for the time being become absorbing.

4 William Shakespeare, *Macbeth*, act 5, scene 5.

In a well-known passage in his autobiography, J. S. Mill records how he went through a period of deep depression as a young man. He had been brought up to suppose that the betterment of society and the good of mankind were the objects of existence, and the source of human happiness. He was still intellectually convinced that these were the values he should pursue, but he did not feel any interest in them. At the depth of his depression, the thought that tormented him was that pleasures were all of them exhaustible. Even music, from which he had always gained the greatest pleasure, seemed liable to come to an end. 'The octave', he wrote 'consists only of five notes and two semi-tones, which can be put together in only a limited number of ways; most of these, it seemed to me, must already have been discovered, and there could not be room for a long succession of Mozarts or Webers to strike out, as these had done, entirely new and surpassingly rich veins of musical beauty.'[5] It was at this stage that he first read Wordsworth's poems, and he records 'In them I seemed to draw from a Source of inward joy, of sympathetic and imaginative pleasure, which could be shared by all human beings. ... From them I seemed to learn what would be the perennial sources of happiness, when all the greater evils of life shall have been removed.'[6] He had come across something at last which seemed infinite and which could never be used up, and this was the insight provided by the imagination itself. Arguing about this later with a friend, who thought such imaginative pleasures unreal, he said, 'It was in vain that I urged on him that the imaginative emotion which an idea, when vividly conceived, excites in us, is not an illusion but a fact.'[7]

This phrase is worth considering further. 'The imaginative emotion which an idea, when vividly conceived, excites in us' is not only, as Mill said, real, but it is of intrinsic value. There is no need to ask what it is valuable *for*. It is like health; something which everyone knows is worth having for its own sake. Once it is experienced, it is desired; without it, there is the danger of the boredom and apathy which characterises so many children,

5  John Stuart Mill, *Autobiography* (London: Longmans, Green, Reader, & Dyer, 1873), p. 145.

6  Mill, *Autobiography*, p. 148.

7  Mill, *Autobiography*, p. 151.

and which may become particularly prevalent during adolescence. In the 1970s an English teacher from Bristol called Michael Paffard wrote two remarkable books, called *Inglorious Wordsworths* and *The Unattended Moment*, in which he explored what may be called epiphanies, or moments of intense significance, experienced by children and adolescents.[8] In the first book he records the outcome of a questionnaire he distributed among his pupils, getting them to describe their own experiences; in the second he put together accounts of such experiences recorded in autobiographies. I will quote from just one such account, in this case of a childhood experience; it comes from the autobiography of René Cutforth.[9] He was entirely bored at his prep school at the age of eleven; maths, history, science, cricket all left him with nothing except a vague anxiety, and then:

> It happened on a run. The weather was so bad at the beginning of that term that cricket was impossible, so after lunch we all sloshed off in the rain in a straggling column across country, shepherded by Mr Johnson, an unhappy intellectual to whom these chores fell as by some natural law. After about a mile and a half I was leaning against a gate between two sodden lengths of cow pasture, getting my breath back, when I suddenly saw in the scuffed mud patch under the gate a piece of stone washed clear by the rain, and, contained in it, an intricate and perfect ribbed coil, like a coiled-up snake, in a sort of dull gold. It was a beautiful object and a splendid find, and I was just wondering whether I could possibly carry it back, or should I hide it somewhere to be recovered on Sunday when I didn't have to run, when Mr Johnson appeared, more than half inclined to lean on the same gate and get his breath back. 'Oh sir,' I said, 'what's this?' 'That's an ammonite,' said Mr Johnson, puffing and blowing, 'a fossil shell. Very old, used to live here when all this land was under the sea, a long time ago.' 'Before the Romans and Ancient Britons?'

---

8 Michael Paffard, *Inglorious Wordsworths: A Study of Some Transcendental Experiences in Childhood and Adolescence* (London: Hodder & Stoughton, 1973); *The Unattended Moment: Excerpts from Autobiographies with Hints and Guesses* (London: SCM Press, 1976).

9 René Cutforth, *Order to View* (London: Faber & Faber, 1969).

I asked. 'Oh long before, about sixty million years ago, before there were any men at all', he said. 'At least I think that's right. They seem to change the estimate about every five years.' 'Sixty million years old? Before or after the world was made in six days?' 'Well metaphorically,' Mr Johnson said, 'about the Thursday of that week. An interesting period geologically: the giant lizards, the dinosaurs, the pterodactyls ... they're all still here under the ground. This part of England is full of them.' I don't know why this revelation of the huge continuity of the past should have been such a release to my imagination, but it was. It was a genuine illumination: something to do with perspective, something to do with the mysterious quality of time itself. Something to do with buried treasure, something which joined the separate worlds of poetry and finding out and learning and digging and the splendid look of the country. Something that put cricket in its pettifogging place. During that summer I seldom emerged from the Jurassic age. I found a quarry full of ammonites and belemnites and terebratulae and thyconellae and rhynconellae and gryphaea and pecten and sea-urchins. A whole sea-bottom of creatures who'd lived and died and left themselves to be explained. This was the point ... before any could possibly have explained them. With great difficulty I read that whole book, the *Origin of the Species*. I sent for everything the South Kensington Museum had published about the Jurassic and the lower Lias. I knew the names of all the creatures.

On this passage, Michael Paffard comments:

Whether intentionally or by accident, the weedy Mr Johnson had held the murmuring shell of time to his ear, and kindled a spark of romance a sense of wonder. When he stopped by the gate in the rain and talked to the small boy instead of telling him to 'cut along' he was TEACHING and anything less important than that is called teaching only by courtesy.

It is because children and adolescents, despite their often glazed and sulky exterior, are many of them capable of such awakenings, are capable of crazes, when they are in the grip of which the subject of the craze seems infinite and unlimited, that teachers have a duty to try to jolt them out of apathy, to cause them to feel the excitement of which J. S. Mill spoke. And this is the education of the imagination. It opens the eyes and ears of the pupils to values which can be shared, and which, even if they are not universally shared, are worth pursuing for their own sake, are of intrinsic worth.

In all such imaginative awakening, artistic or scientific, I believe there is a sense of continuity with both past and future. Children have to learn that where they are now is not the only place: that if they learn about the past or the present, the narrative is not closed. Our sense of time, both past and future, separates us from other animals. It is only human beings who can place themselves in a continuous context of values, in which what is liked and disliked, feared, admired or despised can be articulated and handed on, not simply through the genes, but by discussion and dialogue, by the actual practice of painting pictures, or performing and composing music, with the established trust and benevolent influence of a teacher. It is through this kind of articulated value-system that human beings can come to regard their lives as having significance.

And so we come to music education, in which is a crucial part of the education of the imagination. There are three aspects of musical education, all equally to be described as the education of the imagination, that I shall touch on, though far from adequately. The first is the development of what may be called musical skills. It is a part of the human imagination that it allows us to embrace the concept of what can be done, not necessarily by ourselves, but by others. There is probably nobody now who does not believe that the skills of reading and calculating are both obviously useful, and indeed necessary to as many children as can possibly acquire them. But they are more than this: they open up worlds closed to those who do not possess these skills. Although there doubtless exist talented natural musicians who, as it were, live by their ears, yet it is my opinion that a child who is not taught to read music is shut off from enormous areas of pleasure and understanding; and that the parallel between reading words and reading musical notation is quite close. Both may be taught to most people without too much difficulty; and both should be taught when the pupil is quite young. But reading music is, of course, only one small part of the skills that music education should teach, and not the most important. In teaching even quite small children to play musical instruments (and even quite simple instruments) the teacher will be opening up for them the idea of doing something well, doing it properly, which is in itself an imaginative opening. As soon as a child starts to learn to play, for example, the violin, and to listen to other people playing the violin, she will begin to see, however obscurely, what infinite possibilities the instrument has, what infinitely many ways there are in which, if she becomes keen on it, she may improve her own playing, how infinitely far she has to go. This may of course be simply depressing; not everyone is cut out to enjoy playing the violin. But a good teacher will at least make her, the pupil, feel that she can do today things she could not do yesterday, and this in itself can be an approach to Mill's 'imaginative emotion', and will be such, if the child has a natural affinity with the instrument. So the first aspect of music education that is capable in itself of engaging children's imagination and laying the foundation for imaginative non-boredom in the future is the teaching of skills or techniques.

A second aspect (which will, indeed, chronologically come first and is of the greatest importance) is the communicative and co-operative aspect of music, which makes education in it of irreplaceable value. At a very simple level, musicians learn a kind of inner discipline. They learn when they are small children to move rhythmically to a dance tune or a march, to clap rhythmically in a particular time, to sing in tune (more or less) and in time. To learn this is, again, to learn a skill, to understand what is possible in the way of controlling your own movements, and your own responses. And such discipline becomes the foundation of using music expressively and hearing it as expressive. This kind of learning can start long before school age. Indeed, it is impossible to exaggerate the value to any child that it should. In the present climate of interest in what children's pre-school needs are, music has not been much mentioned. But it should be; and it is timely to remark here on the enormously important role that radio specifically for children should have, to be listened to both at home and at nursery school or playgroup. Radio, of course, is not just for music. Children could learn to count, to recognise letters, to recite the alphabet through radio, as well. But it is also an obvious easy way to introduce songs and rhymes, rhythms, and that 'joining in', which crucially bring a sense of a point – a telos – to a young child's life. It is much to be hoped that, at last, in the context of their own Good Start Initiative[10] and the new emphasis on early learning, the Government will look with favour on allocating a frequency for such a radio station, which is now virtually ready and waiting to start. It is disgraceful to argue, as the BBC has, that children do not like radio. They would like it, and we it, if they were offered it as part of their daily life.

As things are, I believe that a lot of children suffer serious deprivation if they do not have a teacher who can make singing in class a regular element in their education. The combination of words with music is one of the most natural sources of human pleasure, and one of the most profound. It is partly that both words and music are most easily grasped as expressive when conjoined. It is partly too that in a song the words take on a new significance, and the concept of music-making as a co-operative activity first dawns on a child in class singing. One of my daughters, a musician, but not a professional teacher, runs a music club once a week in her daughter's primary school (and I can foresee will continue to run it long after her daughter has left). My daughter told me about the amazed excitement of the children when they first began to be competent enough to sing rounds and canons. The idea that between them, just by sticking to their part, they could produce such harmonies was profoundly new for them, and a matter of great pride. So they demanded that they be allowed to make up their own words, even to some of the melancholy rounds she mostly taught them. And most of the words proclaimed that they, the singers, were the greatest. It is a matter of regret that not every primary school can afford to have at least one member of staff who is a competent accompanist, and who understands the things one can get children to experience through singing. After all, this is a musical education which is free, once the member of staff has been employed; there is no need to hire or borrow or buy an instrument, no need to charge parents for lessons outside the curriculum. Radio in this context can to some extent make good the absence of a musically confident teacher.

10 Department of Education, Northern Ireland, *Report by the Education and Training Inspectorate on the Making A Good Start Initiative, Inspected 1996–8* (Bangor, Co. Down: Education and Training Inspectorate, 1999).

It is through the combination of words with music that many people who would not describe themselves as particularly 'musical' experience the most profound imaginative pleasure in music. For there is a sense in which all music is 'mood music'; and in songs this may become most manifest. One has only to think, for example, of Schubert's *Winterreise*, or Britten's *Serenade for Tenor, Horn and Strings*.

In the case of any music that has been written down, there is an intrinsic sense of continuity and yet novelty in its performance. It is being reproduced, reinterpreted, but it carries (unless it is a brand new piece, in which case it carries only promise) a sense of its past, and past performances. Nowhere is this more crucial to the imaginative experience of the music than in church music. Ancient ecclesiastical buildings, old orders of worship, music written for use in services and so used for centuries, may evoke a sense of permanence and a living continuity with the past which is, or ought to be, the life of Christianity and of most formal religions. Such consciousness of continuity is an essentially imaginative experience, and it is not separable from that human sympathy, the understanding of how other humans think and thought, which can make us grasp as other animals cannot, that humans are all in the same boat – a boat that has, precariously, been afloat for centuries.

And here I must return briefly to the thought that when schools are ordered to teach 'values', though this is often thought of in terms of moral values, it must be remembered that there are what may roughly be called aesthetic values as well, which require imagination for their recognition and acceptance even more obviously, perhaps, than do moral values. And yet the difference between the aesthetic and the moral is seldom easy to draw; nor is it necessary to try too hard to draw it. At any rate whenever the Church has made efforts to exclude the aesthetic from its rituals, to separate the pleasurable from the elevating or morally instructive, it has always failed to a greater or lesser degree. The Church has always had an ambivalent attitude towards imagination, setting it in contrast with that revelation supposed to be the only source of truth. The pleasures of the imagination, derived characteristically from poetry, painting and music, however deep such pleasures may be, have always been taken as pleasures to be forgone if they stood in the way of salvation by pure faith or pure works. A more practical, non-aesthetic approach to the gospels has again and again been demanded, not an imaginative grasp of the story – a response which is after all as appropriate to fiction as to fact. There have therefore been frequent demands to go back to the gospels without the thought of symbolism, without extravagant ceremonies, without elaborate music. The result of these efforts in the past has generally been to change but not to destroy the central role that the aesthetic imagination must play in the contemplation of Christian dogma. We have only to think of the translation of the Latin services into the vernacular to see how the poetic genius of the English of that time, the national ear for linguistic rhythms peculiarly strong in the sixteenth century, was called upon in aid to produce a liturgy now often castigated for being too poetic. Again, the Council of Trent laid down clear guidelines for the setting of sacred texts to music, specifying one note to each syllable with no ornamentation or other purely musical embellishments.

The outcome was not austerity or poverty of imagination, but an outburst of the most superb church music ever composed. What came about was a new interpretation of the texts, a new understanding of them precisely through the music to which they were set. The challenge laid down by the Council of Trent was to think of the texts afresh, and it is as if there was new music waiting to be written in response to the challenge. The outcome was music of such genius (think, for example, of the great verse anthems of Orlando Gibbons) that it is impossible to listen to it without thinking through it of the significance of the words. Such of course had been the intention of those who ordained the change; but they could have had no idea of the miraculous creativity of those who set themselves to obey the instructions. Such a happy miscalculation was possible for two reasons, both relevant to the theme of the imagination. First, while all poetry suggests more than it says, songs, as I have said, especially express more than could be translated into what plain words could convey. Secondly, it is in my view the death of religion to try to state literally what is being said. Religious ideas must always be expressed through metaphor and symbol, words themselves being inadequate to the task, when literally understood. And this is exactly the kind of meaning which music is especially fitted to convey and to enhance.

And so I have already begun to speak of the third aspect of musical education which I undertook to come to, and it is ultimately the most important. Children must be given the chance to experience music as an imaginative creation which goes beyond words, as a means of communication which may take over where words cannot be found. This is the profound value of music, an intrinsic value, not pursued or loved for the sake of anything else, but for itself. It may be argued that what I am speaking of is, after all, only a pleasure. Education, and all the vast resources that are put into it cannot be supposed to be in the end only for the sake of pleasure. But such an argument is I believe profoundly mistaken. I admit that pleasure in music is only one among the pleasures that human beings can experience, though an important one. But that it is a pleasure does not, in my view, entail that it cannot be one of the aims of education. Imaginative pleasures, whether in science, the natural world, mathematics, history or literature, are the goals towards which teachers should aim, as well as the pleasures of problem-solving or of technological invention. The ideally good education is an education which leads to enjoyment; and enjoyment, the sense of excitement of which Mill spoke, is precisely the gift of the imagination. It may also be argued that not everyone enjoys music, and so time and money should not be squandered on an aspect of education that will be rejected by a high proportion of those who are subjected to it. But I believe that this argument too is mistaken. Most people naturally enjoy music, many regard it as a necessary background to their everyday activities. Education in music from an early age can only enhance their pleasure, and render them more aware of the role that music plays in their lives.

To deprive those people whose pleasure in music may become central to their imaginative lives if it is encouraged, on the grounds that not everyone will share their pleasure, is irresponsible. Music education used to be thought of as largely a matter of imposing from the outside a 'canon' of Western, mostly European, music on those for whom it was an alien form. Those days are now over. It is recognised that there are many musical traditions to which children should be introduced. The active engagement in music from pre-school days onwards can bear fruit later, whatever the origins or the style of music it may lead to. Equally irresponsible is the idea that music education should be confined to those who may become professionals. As G. K. Chesterton put it: 'If a thing's worth doing, it's worth doing badly.'[11] We should bear in mind the great tradition of British amateur music – choirs, chamber groups, orchestras and brass bands. Such amateurs provide a background against which alone professionals can emerge and concert-halls be filled. Moreover, amateur music-making is above all one of the factors which can give significance to people's lives. The well-known thought that music is a common language also has relevance here. In the precarious boat we are in we need everything we get in the way of shared or potentially shared experiences. This is, perhaps, what our imagination is really for.

11 G K. Chesterton, *What's Wrong with the World* (1910), end of chapter 14.

*Second Bernarr Rainbow Lecture, given at
the Royal Society of Arts, 8 John Adam
Street, London, 23 October 2000*

# Music and Education:
# Towards a Non-Philistine Society

## LORD MOSER

Claus Moser, KCB, CBE, was created a Baron of Regent's Park in the London Borough of Camden in 2001. He was born in Berlin, studied at the London School of Economics and taught there, specialising in Social Statistics. He has been Chairman of the British Museum Development Trust (1993–2003); Chancellor of the Open University of Israel (1994–2004); and Chairman of Askonas-Holt Ltd (1990–2002). He was Warden of Wadham College, Oxford, from 1984 to 1993, and served prominently on many committees covering a variety of subjects, including music. He was knighted in 1973. He is also a capable pianist, and at a recent count he had nineteen honorary degrees.

## ■ The arts at the centre

As I was thinking about this lecture, my mind kept going back to childhood in Berlin. Inevitably my main thought was of the beginnings of one of the most evil times in history – which none of us can ever forget. But I also remember with gratitude that it was in those years that my lifelong passion for music took root. In the 1920s and pre-Hitler's 1930s, there was probably no other country as culture-rich as Germany. Berlin's musical life was exciting beyond belief, and any child with the slightest interest in great music had a wonderful time.

I was certainly lucky to grow up in a family devoted to music. But that was not all. In school, from about age four onwards, music was a central activity. That was taken for granted, and it mirrored a society in which the arts had, throughout history, occupied a place in the sun.

Then Hitler picked the arts out for early attack, partly because they were provocative and daring. Also many Jews were involved and from 1933 Hitler removed them from the public arts. But such was the passion for culture within the Jewish community that the Kulturbund was established in which only Jews could perform. That is where I had my earliest great musical experiences. On coming to England in 1936, I was lucky to go to Frensham Heights, a school devoted to music. From then onwards my life has been constantly enriched by music. The German philosopher Nietzsche once said that 'Life without music would be a mistake.'[1] I am happy to say that this is one mistake I have not made. I have played the piano, and had close involvements, above all with the Royal Opera House, but also with Glyndebourne, the London Symphony Orchestra, festivals, amateur music, music management and much else.

Against that personal background you can imagine that I feel greatly honoured to give a lecture commemorating a man who – passionately and effectively – devoted his life to music education: Bernarr Rainbow, whose long life ended in 1998. He was a fine musician and musicologist and above all a great teacher. Many of his books on music education and its history enriched the lives of teachers and pupils. I do not doubt that his writing and influence will continue to benefit successive generations, helped by the Trust now chaired by Professor Peter Dickinson. I think Bernarr Rainbow would be pleased by current researches on music education, above all here at the RSA in the important work led by Rick Rogers. But he would be less pleased by what is happening on the ground, and probably share my concern that so many – the majority – of today's children will grow up with all too little contact with great music.

I speak with a passionate belief in the enriching force of the arts in the life of each one of us and of society as a whole. For this audience, the case need not be argued. But there are philistines in the wings of today's society, some in high places, who fail to appreciate what the arts bring to a civilised society, to our quality of life. The arts are not marginal, as was well put years ago by President Kennedy: 'The life of the Arts, far from being an interruption, a distraction in the life of the nation, is very close to

---

1 'Ohne Musik wäre das Leben ein Irrtum.' Friedrich Nietzsche, *Götzen-Dämmerung, oder, Wie man mit dem Hammer philosophiert* (1889).

the centre of a nation's purpose, and is a test of a nation's civilisation'.[2] In short, not the icing on the cake, but part of its core. We are a long way from realising that vision.

In my remarks I will focus on music, though much of what I say applies to all art forms. I wish for a society in which every child experiences all kinds of music, and in which classical music is not squeezed to the margin just because it fails in the popularity stakes. And I wish for a society in which philistines, with a disdain for culture, become devoid of relevant influence.

Some years ago, when I was Chairman of the Royal Opera House [1974–87], I made a speech comparing the public support of the arts in this country with the more generous scene amongst our European neighbours. The then Minister of the Arts was asked to comment. He said, in Parliament, that 'We are all used to Claus Moser's annual whingeing for the arts.' I hope for the day when no passionate spokesman for the arts will be criticised for whingeing. Anyhow, today's lecture is not a whinge. I will praise much that is admirable in our musical world and the arts generally, which is one of this country's success stories. But I also have a nagging concern about the future. Unless we achieve a change of climate many of today's children may join the ranks of the philistines.

## ■ A remarkable transformation

But it is only right to set my concerns against the background of the remarkable transformation in the arts we have enjoyed in recent times, not least in music. It is not many decades since this country was known as 'das Land ohne Musik'[3] – an amazing thought when one looks at London today, not to mention the rest of the country. Let me take opera as a brief illustration. Early last century there were the annual seasons created by Sir

---

2 Statement prepared for Creative Arts 1963 and inscribed at the Kennedy Center for Performing Arts.

3 Oskar Adolf Hermann Schmitz, *Das Land ohne Musik* (Munich: G. Müller, 1904). See Boris Johnson, 'A Land without Music? Parry, Holst and Elgar to You, Schmitz', *Daily Telegraph*, 10 October 2006; Bernarr Rainbow, *The Land without Music: Musical Education in England, 1800–1860 and its Continental Antecedents* (London: Novello & Co., 1967); Temperley, p. 153 below.

Thomas Beecham; between 1909 and 1920 he performed many operas new to British ears and eyes. The seasons were social as well as musical events, but they did succeed artistically. Then there was the Carl Rosa Company, and Gilbert and Sullivan. That was largely it. No public subsidy, and in a typical year perhaps audiences of a few tens of thousands.

Now look at today. In London alone, we have the Royal Opera House and English National Opera. Some hundreds of performances annually. There is Glyndebourne, and major opera companies in Scotland and Wales, plus Opera North; many fine smaller companies, professional and amateur, much touring, and programmes ranging from the baroque to the contemporary. And some fine modern composers adding to the repertory. Nationwide, audiences run into millions annually, amounting to perhaps 6 per cent of the adult population. Occasionally, seen and heard by additional millions, there are relays on TV and radio, though more often from abroad. We have performances for children and, as in the splendid Hamlyn weeks at Covent Garden, for total newcomers to opera and ballet. Access has been increased beyond recognition and most major opera companies have active educational departments. In short, here is a nation that a few decades ago limited itself to a few spasmodic weeks of opera for the better-off, and that now brings what Johnson called 'an irrational and exotic entertainment' to millions – though one has to add that, as for music generally, the audiences are largely middle-class, and most of them are over sixty.

The general musical scene is no less remarkable. Take London, for example: the Barbican, South Bank Centre and Wigmore Hall can be relied on for major events nightly, with high standards and often adventurous programmes, focusing on classical music but branching out into world music, popular music, jazz and so on. Outreach and educational activities are commonplace and vital. A broadly similar picture applies throughout the country. Look at Birmingham: its musical life transformed by Simon Rattle, now centred on a fine Symphony Orchestra and the parallel contemporary music group. The transformation in other arts is similar, whether one looks at theatre, literature, dance, architecture, museums and galleries, and the visual arts generally, and wide-ranging festivals everywhere.

Such a transformation does not come about by chance. As I look back over the post-war years, I see two major organisational forces which deserve much of our gratitude.

One is the Arts Council. It was its creation by Lord Keynes in 1946 that put Government subsidy on the map. His mission from the outset was to widen artistic experience, while at the same time raising standards – a noble double aim. In successive years, the Council has had its ups and downs – the ups when its Chairman was passionate and determined, the more so when he had behind him an equally determined Minister; the downs when either fell short. In my years as Chairman of the Opera House, I experienced the whole range. Most discouraging for the arts have been the years when the Arts Council, far from seeing itself as an instrument fighting for the arts, became little more than an outpost of government. The arm's-length role could too easily be eroded. Yet there is no doubt that over the years the Council has helped the arts to flourish. The latest signs, in Arts Council Chairman Gerry Robinson's recent speech, are very encouraging.[4] Less bureaucracy is promised and increasing delegation to the regions. Above all, under-funding has been officially recognised. For the future, much still depends on the Council regaining the vision, determination and arm's-length independence that characterised its great years.

There is no doubt about the other telling influence, not least in music: of course, I refer to the BBC, which helped in bringing great music, and programmes about music, to vast numbers. What comes to mind are the fine years of Huw Wheldon, William Glock, David Attenborough and Humphrey Burton, who through the BBC wonderfully enriched Britain's musical life – on radio, and even on TV. Plus the imaginative leadership of Controllers, latterly John Drummond and Nicholas Kenyon, who have made the Proms into the finest music festival anywhere. So the BBC of those times deserved the gratitude of music-lovers old and new.

I am sometimes asked whether the arts transformation of recent decades was also helped by refugees from Hitler in the 1930s. I do not wish to overstate such 'contributionalism', but one cannot doubt that these influences were helpful in many areas, including science, art history, and the arts generally. In the case of music there are indeed notable

4 Sir Gerry Robinson, chairman of the Arts Council 1998–2004, knighted in 2003.

examples. Take Glyndebourne. Created by the remarkable John Christie, it also owed some of its greatness to two refugees – Fritz Busch and Carl Ebert. There was also Rudolf Bing, who later, in 1947, helped to establish the Edinburgh Festival, to be succeeded in due course by another refugee, Peter Diamand. Other immigrant musicians spring to mind: conductors such as Kubelík, Krips, Rankl, Klemperer and Solti; many instrumentalists, and the Amadeus Quartet, which transformed Britain's chamber-music life. Hans Keller in the BBC had a splendid influence. There were music managements and the world of musicologists and impresarios, all enriched by refugees. Not least, there have been the supporters and audiences. On that score I would risk my statistical reputation, for what it is worth, to claim that the refugees and their descendants have produced quite disproportionate numbers of 'bums on seats' and levels of financial support. And of course I hope that we refugees, young and old, who have been fortunate enough to settle here, have helped to infect British culture with our mid-European musical passions.

Much more could be said about the arts transformations of recent decades – not least that it has continued in the present, in part due to the Government. The present Secretary of State for Culture has a clear devotion to the arts.[5] Chris Smith's presence is noted wherever anything artistic is happening, and a whole stream of helpful initiatives have emerged from his Department, often jointly with David Blunkett's Education Department: National Endowment for Science Technology and the Arts, the Wider Opportunities Fund, instrument grants, a grant to encourage Local Education Authorities' musical activities, the Arts Award and, probably most important, the new National Foundation for Youth Music, are examples. Above all, the Minister has squeezed more money out of the Treasury, a modest increase over the next two years, and a more sizeable growth in three years' time. To add to all this, lotteries are an enormous boon to the arts.

The regained confidence – and, I hope, arm's-length position from Government – of the Arts Council gives cause for optimism. Also, within the BBC, there are encouraging signs from Radio 3 with its excitingly

---

5 Chris Smith, first Secretary of State for Culture, Media and Sport (1997–2001), made Baron Smith of Finsbury in 2005.

diverse musical diet, if not yet on TV. Classic FM spreads music widely. In terms of money, the most encouraging change is the Chancellor's reconstruction of charity giving.[6] These are steps which should help to sustain the musical transformation built up over earlier decades. And, as I shall stress again later, there is a huge interest in music outside the traditional classics to be built on.

## ■ Today's concerns

So, if our musical life is so lively, why do I wish to focus on worries about the future? Is it because I am after all a non-reconstructed whinger?

Not so. Like the two Johns – Drummond and Tusa[7] – I believe that, to put it mildly, complacency is out of place. There remain serious reasons for reminding ourselves how far the arts are from being at the secure centre of our society, certainly as far as the so-called high arts are concerned. In short, we still have some way to go towards a truly non-philistine society.

There are many signs. Why is it that any of us involved in the arts, professionally or otherwise, are constantly having to fight our corner – lobbying, campaigning, and facing critical committees, consultants and the like? Why is it that, on the whole, politicians seem distant, manifesto promises apart, with the arts figuring little in priority commitments? In the recent party conferences, they emerged little in any party leader's speeches. Meanwhile, people working in the arts are often caricatured, rather condescendingly, as 'luvvies', or, by implication, regarded as somewhat selfishly unconcerned with the real world. As John Drummond put it in his Royal Philharmonic Society Lecture: 'Politicians seem to believe that the arts are made up of either hysterical egomaniacs who cannot be trusted, or wimps without managerial skills.'[8]

This last criticism is particularly common. Of course, there have been management crises, many of high profile. But on balance, arts

---

6 Under threat in 2012 but reinstated after an outcry.

7 Sir John Drummond, Controller of BBC Radio 3 (1987–92) and of the Proms until 1995.
  Sir John Tusa, Managing Director of the Barbican Arts Centre (1995–2007).

8 John Drummond, 'Taking Music Seriously', Royal Philharmonic Society Lecture 1998.
  See also Michael Berkeley, 'Public Culture, Private Passions', Royal Philharmonic
  Society Lecture 2002; Peter Maxwell Davies, p. 99 below.

organisations, large and small, are well run – artistically and financially. It is notable that Gerry Robinson, the Arts Council's Chairman, said that, on appointment, he expected to find an inefficient, wasteful, badly run arts sector, but after two years' hard investigation, found the opposite. I hope the Government will heed his remarks. Some of my continuing concerns do relate to money. The arts are funded in a pluralist manner, depending on government, local authorities, business, sponsorship, patronage and, of course, the public. This is a good arrangement. The trouble is that each of these sources is fragile.

Most important is the public sector. Happily, at least in my view, we are committed to the arts' being a matter for public subsidy. Moreover, funding has steadily increased since the last war through successive Arts Councils. But the standstill, beginning in the Thatcher years, caused severe problems from which recovery has inevitably been gradual. What is rarely appreciated is that high standards may take years to reach, but that a severe cut can destroy them overnight. Fortunately, the present Government has ended the standstill and moved financially upwards – most recently in the last comprehensive spending review.

Official statistics on the arts, including funding, are sparse, and need greater priority so that we get a regular understanding of audiences, developments, finance, and so forth. But, it is pretty clear that, compared with leading European countries, our arts remain seriously under-funded. The consequences can be seen in closures, cutbacks, compromised popular programmes, unmeetable pressures on more daring activities, falling standards and pathetic pay. At the same time, there is constant government pressure to enlarge education and outreach activities, while – where relevant – reducing entry or seat prices. These may be laudable aims, but one doesn't need to be a statistician to realise that, without extra money, they may all too easily lead to higher deficits or lower standards.

The National Lottery has been a godsend for the arts, above all in creating fine new facilities. The downside has been the delay in recognising that new buildings are costly to run. Revenue funding is now beginning to figure for lottery support – welcome, if late in the day. But one can never be certain, after years of tough experience, that the arts are a secure Government priority. Too much depends on political attitudes of the day. Let the Government note that we spend perhaps only half as much on the arts, as a proportion of gross domestic product, as most of Europe. I am not going to suggest a specific percentage of GDP that we should hope for – that may not be the most helpful approach. The right course is for the appropriate body – in the present context the Arts Council – to assess in turn each artform for which it is responsible, and its financial needs, and then seek the proper resources. The Council's current approach to regional theatre is exactly right. Now it is the turn of music, including music in education.

Not everything falls to central government. The arts must flourish locally, supported by local pride and local involvement. Think of the transformation in the cultural life of Sheffield, or Birmingham, Salford's Lowry Centre, the forthcoming centre in Gateshead, or dozens of others. There are many cities that would stand high in local arts league tables, but many more in which the arts, not least music, are still all too marginal. It is all somewhat random. So much depends on the accident of personalities and local politicians. Financial pressures hit hard. Three years ago Oxfordshire, under financial pressure, reduced arts funding to zero. Happily it has now been re-established, but the intervening years inevitably caused problems. Nor was Oxfordshire's the only authority that singled the arts out for severe cuts. All authorities should support the arts, and ensure supportive local music services. The Department of Culture's grant to a number of authorities is a signal encouragement, which needs to be followed nationally.

A most encouraging development since the war has been business sponsorship, much helped by ABSA.[9] Without sponsorship, few arts organisations would survive. But again one depends on the attitudes of chairmen, partners, boards and chief executives, and on how well the company is doing. A down-turn and support goes to the wall: British Airways and Marks & Spencer are recent examples. Also fashions change, and I doubt I am being paranoid in detecting a shift in corporate preferences from the arts to community and voluntary causes. The so-called 'One Percent Club' for arts sponsorship must get a new momentum.

9  The Association for Business Sponsorship of the Arts, founded in 1976 as a charity to develop partnerships between cultural organisations and private sector business; now Arts and Business.

In short, all parts of pluralist funding are fragile. What musical activities, indeed all arts, need is well-grounded – not luxurious – adequacy of funding and, above all, stability. Ultimately, that depends on the Arts Council, centrally and regionally.

Nor is it only a question of money. The media are crucial. We could do with more newspaper coverage for pieces about music and the other arts. The *New York Times* would be my model. The importance of broadcasting, radio and TV, cannot be exaggerated. In recent years the BBC seemed to retreat massively from the arts, certainly on TV. Hopefully, its promised special arts channel, plus the new commercial arts channel, will lead to a new future. It depends on the power of non-philistines in high broadcasting places.

The concerns I have noted have one thing in common. This is that they reflect national values and ideologies. In spite of the transformation about which I have spoken, I still doubt Britain's true cultural commitment. We still seem too easily influenced by doubts, deeply rooted in history, about the importance of cultural values and activities. There are too many who regard the arts as relatively unimportant, which was surely at the back of Benjamin Britten's mind when he said: 'The average Briton thought, and still thinks, of the Arts as suspect and expensive luxuries'.[10] Such attitudes are indeed deep seated. One cannot avoid noting a certain suspicion of intellectuals, of creativity, of abstract ideas – very different, for example, from our French cousins. The phrase 'too clever by half' is peculiarly British. Where this comes from would demand a lecture in itself. But one can recognise, even today, the Britain which earlier this century displeased the European writer Stefan Zweig.[11] When he came to London he sensed a certain cold reaction to matters cultural and intellectual, and a separateness of intellectuals and artists from society at large.

Perhaps there is another element encouraging negative attitudes. The arts contain elements of provocation and disturbance, often questioning accepted attitudes and lines. They are not necessarily, or even desirably,

---

10 Benjamin Britten, 'On Receiving the First Aspen Award', in *Britten on Music*, ed. Paul Kildea (Oxford: Oxford University Press, 2003), p. 258.

11 Stefan Zweig (1881–1942), Austrian writer who came to London with his second wife in 1934, left in 1940, and died in Brazil.

'politically correct'. Perhaps this is the reason why governments are so readily impatient with creative institutions such as the BBC, the Arts Council, and individual arts organisations. I can't resist quoting Peter Hall's vivid description of a talk with Mrs Thatcher when she was Prime Minister:

> It was like talking to a suspicious headmistress who feared that artiness among the boys and girls might lead to softness and possible left-wing tendencies; they should all aim to get a proper job instead.

I do not wish to overstate the influence of philistines in today's society. But they do remain, and help to shape attitudes. At the worst they fail to realise that a civilised society demands fine culture at its core.

And that leads to another point. It will be obvious that my remarks relate to classical music rather than popular music, world music, rock or jazz. Popular music deserves its name, and will always give pleasure to millions, far more than even the finest classics. It is a matter of taste. Like many others, I think that great classical music has a deeper, more lasting and more totally involving enrichment of one's life than other kinds of music. That is a personal preference, a value judgement. My worry is simply that the forces backing popular culture may come to marginalise the less popular; that the influences of government, politics, TV and radio, education, the newspapers, may become too driven by populism. All music is exciting and deserving of encouragement. All types of music have things in common, and one kind can often open the door to others. I passionately want to ensure that the doors to classical music are kept widely ajar.

Jennie Lee, when she was Arts Minister many years ago, said: 'If children at an early age became accustomed to the arts as part of everyday life, they are more likely in maturity first to accept and then to demand them.'[12] And in our own time, David Blunkett, Secretary of State for Education and Employment, said: 'Music is a vital part of every child's education and plays an important part in this country's culture.'

---

12 Jennie Lee, Minister for the Arts in Harold Wilson's government from 1964–70,
   created Baroness Lee of Ashridge in 1970.

That, indeed, is the proper vision. But how do we get there? The RSA's new report *Regenerating the Arts in Schools* sets out the challenges, as does the report of the National Advisory Committee on Cultural and Creative Education, chaired by Professor Ken Robinson.[13]

Take primary schools. This is where, hopefully following lively music in nursery years, enthusiasm should be kindled and developed. Many schools do have splendid music activities, but if the Head is less than enthusiastic, music becomes at best marginal. This is especially a risk in disadvantaged communities with probably less parental concern. Much local authority support has disappeared, or been cut; and the moratorium (due to the necessary introduction of the literacy hour) in the last two years has further marginalised the subject. Many schools have long given it low priority, and more do so now. It is a depressing picture.

Now that the subject is at least formally back in the curriculum, everything must be done to ensure that it regains a proper place, not least in poor environments. This is the moment for Government to convince all primary schools that music is a vital subject for children, and indeed for the life of the school; to disseminate models of good practice; to ensure good teaching; to make instrumental teaching free again; and to provide the necessary resources nationally. The Government's important new National Foundation for Youth Music can help in this process.

It has long been a regrettable fact that, in secondary schools, children can proceed without studying any humanities or arts. This would be unthinkable in most European countries, and should be unthinkable here. As a result, many – perhaps most – children grow up hardly encountering classical music. They are indeed surrounded by music – on radio, film, internet and elsewhere, but it is its place in schools that matters above all for understanding and discriminating between different kinds of music. The new Harland report *Arts Education in Secondary Schools: Effects and Effectiveness*, sponsored by the RSA and the Arts Council, provides the facts and points the way.[14] We are reminded of the great, and unacceptable,

13 Published, respectively, as: Royal Society of Arts, *Regenerating the Arts in Schools* (London: RSA, 2000); *All our Futures: Creativity, Culture and Education* (London: DfEE Publications, 1999).

14 John Harland *et al.*, *Arts Education in Secondary Schools: Effects and Effectiveness* (Slough: National Foundation for Education Research, 2000).

variety between schools in what they provide. A child may strike lucky or not, depending on the enthusiasm of the Head and his or her staff, local backing, and above all the quality of teaching. Teaching in many schools is extremely poor. No wonder that so many pupils report lack of interest or, believe it or not, even of enjoyment of music. Most striking, music emerges as 'the most problematic and vulnerable artform' in school.[15] It is a sad picture, confirming my concerns for the future.

What emerges from all studies is the serious teacher situation. Taking the arts generally, teacher recruitment has continued to fall – from 1997/8, when it was 16 per cent under need, to 23 per cent under need in 1998/9. Teacher training colleges have increasingly marginalised the arts, especially music. Teaching is often done by unqualified teachers, particularly worrying in music where a specialist background is so important. This is the single most urgent area for improvement. We need a proper place for the arts in all initial teacher training, in-service and career development opportunities, special qualifications, and teacher links with the arts. Not least, all Heads should be trained in arts education. I hope that the Teacher Training Agency will be given every support, with the necessary resources, to correct a disgraceful blot on arts education.

In sum, to achieve our vision, music and other arts should be enabled to find a proper place in flexible curricula, in out-of-school activities, and in informal education after school. Inspection by properly qualified inspectors needs to be ensured. The re-establishment of peripatetic music teaching advisory services, instrumental grants, and arrangements for musicians in residence, should be local aims throughout the country.

In case it is necessary to stress, I am thinking of all kinds of music, but with classical music at the centre, and with all children in mind, not just those with special talents. They all deserve entry to the magical world of music – playing, singing, listening, composing and, above all, participating. I know this already happens in many schools. Which only makes me sadder that it doesn't happen routinely in all.

Much will depend on the local community. Schools after all are not isolated institutions. To bring about a lively arts activity, the school will need enthusiastic support of the local authority, companies, shops,

15 Harland *et al.*, *Arts Education in Secondary Schools*, pp. 567–8.

voluntary organisations and, above all, from those involved in the arts. The Arts Council, with the Qualifications and Curriculum Authority, has set out a procedure for creating partnerships, and Chris Smith has announced grants for twelve Creative Partnerships. What is crucial is that such partnerships are based on the arts themselves – orchestras, museums, theatres and so forth. The arts must be at the centre, not a separate, sometimes off-putting, sector.

Community arts developments are, to my mind, the most promising. Arts-related partnerships have emerged in, for example, Bristol and Sheffield, to mention only two. To take a less prosperous location – and I hope I do not embarrass my son, who carries a major responsibility for it – I will quote Morecambe. Thanks to the support of the Northern Regional Arts Board, and local vision, music is becoming more and more part of its life. It is brought into schools through 'More Music in Morecambe', ensuring that the children encounter a wide range of music of all kinds, not least classical.[16] Indeed, world music, jazz, rock – all kinds of popular music – may well be the right entrance door. There are bands in the streets, choral events, every encouragement for young and old to participate together. Gradually enthusiasm spreads, and space is carved out, above all in and around schools, and music becomes part of Morecambe's life. Many models like Morecambe exist for others to follow. For guidance one can also turn to the exciting work of the Centre for Creative Communities, as also to the Arts Council and the Culture Department. Some of the new initiatives, such as local authority grants, the Wider Opportunities initiative, and the National Endowment for Science Technology and the Arts, will all help in the same direction.

In community arts, schools and the arts themselves must jointly be at the centre. I would like to see every community in the country progressing in this way, with national, regional and local support, not least from the business world. But community arts require properly trained leaders. At present too few are available, and this is a priority role for further education, and teacher training colleges and specialist music colleges. I

---

16 More Music in Morecambe, a community music and educational charity based at The Hothouse, established in 1993.

would particularly like the music colleges to embrace training for music teachers, and community musicians, in their priorities.

In the community context, I particularly applaud the creation by the Culture Secretary of the National Foundation for Youth Music. It focuses on the under-eighteens and works precisely in the directions I have indicated. The challenge is how to ensure that its influence moves into a national programme to benefit millions of children. It must show how to build on one-off and pilot initiatives with that in mind.

I have mentioned only a few changes necessary to move the arts towards centre stage in our educational scene. The challenges are set out fully in the report *All our Futures*, in which we looked at the arts in the wider context of creativity. The initial Government response was disappointing, but some of the new initiatives show the report's influence. If our key educational recommendations are implemented, a promising future will emerge. The report by the think-tank Demos, also dealing with creativity, and the latest RSA report on *The Disappearing Arts* all point in the same direction.[17] No more reports are needed. Only action.

## ■ A change of climate

To conclude, let me quote Confucius: 'Music produces a kind of pleasure which human nature cannot do without.' Not only pleasure and happiness. It can move one beyond words, uplift one's spirits, excite, console, and heal – there is almost nothing it cannot do. For me, all this has been achieved by classical music, and this lecture has expressed my wish for this experience to be spread widely, for young and old. Really no words can express it all. As George Steiner once wrote: 'For music puts our being as men and women in touch with that which transcends the sayable and which outstrips the analysable.' And every hope I have expressed points to the same thing: the need for a changed climate surrounding the arts, not least music. That depends on funding improvements and stability from government and local government; the courage of the BBC to give high culture its due, not least with an educational slant; the willingness of

17 Rick Rogers, *The Disappearing Arts: The Current State of the Arts in Initial Teacher Training and Professional Development* (London: Royal Society of Arts, 1998).

sponsors, corporate and individual, to back the arts alongside other worthy claimants; crucial advances in the arts within education; the continued enthusiasm of the arts themselves to devote their energies to education and community involvement; community arts partnerships everywhere; and, last but not least, public enthusiasm.

For leadership towards a changed climate one must look to government. And there the desired steps are many. Some are small, even if important. For example, let the word 'élitist' disappear from government pronouncements, except as praise for high artistic achievements. Let the emphasis on educational, outreach priorities stop; not because it is not important, but on the contrary because arts organisations have treated it as such for years, with resounding impact. Let the Government accept – especially since the Arts Council Chairman has so clearly remarked on it – that, on the whole, arts organisations are skilfully and efficiently run. And let it therefore be accepted that, even though people from the business world often have much to contribute to governing arts bodies, the precondition for their involvement must be passion for the relevant art, and commitment to it. Let it also be accepted that arts organisations flourish best if they can focus on their artistic work without excessive bureaucratic interruption, which can easily leave the arts themselves out of sight. Of course, where government money is involved, accountability is right and necessary. But accountability does not mean control – an ever-present temptation for governments. Which is why an arm's-length Arts Council is so vital.

One cannot say often enough that the arts, not least music, are central to a truly civilised society. They are what makes a nation great, and what remains in the historic mind long after industries, economic ups and downs, even governments are forgotten. Everyone with influence should be proud to remind the nation how much is owed to the splendour of our arts. And, as the Prime Minister said in the remark I quoted earlier, they are part of a better new society. The opportunity is there to grasp.

I wish this vision to be symbolised by the actions of our political leaders, their participation in all kinds of artistic, not least musical, events and their visible commitment. I wish the arts to figure not only in specific initiatives (which I very much support), but in national programmes bringing benefits disproportionate to their cost and enhancing the lives of today's children for the future. And let the emphasis, passionate and committed, be on the wonders of the arts as such, even though creative industries, social engineering and economic benefits are valuable by-products. 'Arts for Arts' sake' is the motto.

So I hope for a change of climate, a change of mood. I want classical music, along with music generally, to enrich the lives of millions, as it has mine. I want to ensure that we do not turn more children into adult philistines through gaps in our educational arrangements. I believe that education is at the heart of most things. Like many people I am delighted that the Prime Minister has committed himself to three major priorities: 'Education, Education, Education'.[18] My hope is that he will attach to one of these 'Es' a little suffix 'a', meaning that it stands for Education for the Arts.

## ■ Postscript, December 2010

If I were to give this lecture now, ten years on, would my central message be similar? In a sense, yes. I would want to convey my passion for the arts, again quoting President Kennedy:

> The life of the arts, far from being an interruption or distraction in the life of the nation, is very close to the centre of the nation's purpose, and is a test of a nation's civilisation.

Now, as a decade ago, I would want to give credit to many achievements in this country's art world. But also, even more than a decade ago, I would want to stress my deep concern about what is lacking. Now, as then, there are too many philistines in high place: in government, in industry and business, in the media, even in education, where attitudes and interests of the young are formed.

When I gave the original lecture, I noted that funding of the arts was a pluralist matter, depending on government, local authorities, business sponsorship, patronage and, of course, the public – with the public sector the most important. In those days we could happily count on public subsidy. Speaking in 2010, I would not find such confidence. Of course, we are in critical economic times. But there is no escaping the clear signs that, in

---

18 Manifesto pledge by Tony Blair, British Prime Minister 1997–2007.

the current coalition government's spending cuts, the arts have drawn a particularly harsh lot. Apart from a few leading arts institutions, mainly in London, the rest face an unprecedentedly tough future, especially if they are north of Birmingham and, in general, small enterprises. The government urges philanthropists to fill the gap, without introducing any helpful tax reforms.

My belief in the importance of the arts as totally central to our quality of life and economic prosperity remains as passionate now as ten years ago, but my heart is heavy about the outlook they face.

## ■ Post-postscript, January 2013

What now strikes me more than ever before is how much has indeed been achieved, in spite of everything, in raising our standards in classical music – and not only standards, but range of activities too. This can be attributed in part to private philanthropy, and also to the extraordinary motivation and energy of those in charge of our orchestras, chamber music groups, opera houses and other performing venues. There is much to be proud of, which makes it even more worrying that the current government is sidelining music in our schools.[19]

---

19 See 'Wilful Exclusion from the Arts?', joint letter to *The Times*, 16 January 2013.

*Third Bernarr Rainbow Lecture, given
at the Guildhall School of Music and
Drama, London, 17 October 2001*[1]

# Music in the School Curriculum: Why Bother?

JOHN PAYNTER

John Paynter (1931–2010) was born in London, studied at Trinity College of
Music, and then took a DPhil at the University of York in 1971. He became
a lecturer there under Wilfrid Mellers in 1969, and went on to hold the
professorship from 1982 to 1997. He taught in a variety of schools and,
through his books, articles and lectures, became an international authority
on school music, in particular doing pioneering work in composition and
creative music-making. Paynter was also a composer. He gained the OBE
in 1985.

IN SPITE OF CENTURIES of experience and experiment, the
practicalities and benefits of general education – schooling – remain
uncertain. Can we sustain the spread of subjects that now make up the
curriculum? In particular, can we justify time spent on music, which to
many would appear to be a specialised study for the talented? The evidence
of past practice suggests that the content of classroom music teaching has
not done much to help the majority of people to understand music. Yet
making music is manifestly an important feature of our humanity. Are
there principles at work deep in the nature of music which explain this,
and can those features be exploited as the basis of a musical education
which will have value for everyone?

In his *English Social History* George Trevelyan revealed a disappointment
with formal education. It had, he said, 'produced a vast population able
to read but unable to distinguish what is worth reading' (1942, p. 582).
Twenty-two years later the American psychologist B. F. Skinner, writing in
*New Scientist*, suggested that 'Education is what survives when what has

---

[1] Variants of this lecture were published in Italian as 'Sull'insegnamento della musica
nei programme scolastici', in *beQuadro* 77/79 (2002), pp. 5–13; and in the *British
Journal of Music Education* 19.3 (2002), pp. 215–26.

been learnt has been forgotten' (1964, p. 484) – a maxim echoed in his book *The Technology of Teaching*, where he asserts that 'one of the ultimate advantages of an education is simply coming to the end of it' (Skinner, 1968, p. 148).

So much, then, for 'schooling'; for that is what Trevelyan and Skinner had in mind: not an abstract theory of education but the practicalities of the curriculum. In effect they both seem to have been suggesting that school probably does not do us much harm but neither does it do us a great deal of good. How, then, can we justify the content of the school curriculum? Should it include anything other than the basic skills of literacy and numeracy? And if there should be other subjects, can we justify time spent on music? Does music have identifiable educational benefit?

### ■ Knowledge and understanding

The word 'curriculum' suggests 'a course to be run'; a voyage of discovery, perhaps – although in practice the emphasis has tended to be on the challenge rather than on the experience. A curriculum very easily becomes a summary of knowledge to be passed on, established skills to be acquired and well-attested facts to be memorised. Thus Roger Ascham (1570/1927, p. 25) in the late sixteenth century:

> After the childe hath learned perfitlie the eight partes of speach, let him then learne the right joyning togither of substantives and adjectiues, the nowne with the verbe, the relatiue with the antecedent.

Applied to schooling, prescribed learning became the norm, notwithstanding other possibilities demonstrated by visionary teachers such as Pestalozzi (1746–1827) and Froebel (1782–1852), who believed that it was important to build upon pupils' experiences and personal discoveries (cf. Rainbow, 1989, p. 135; Kendall, 1986). Given the incidence of reforming views, it is, perhaps, surprising that legislation in nineteenth-century England enacting 'universal education' merely reinforced the tendency to prescription and conformity. Clearly the notion of 'education for all' implied that the school curriculum should be *accessible to all pupils*, but often that was achieved by reducing everything to mechanical tasks which could be practised by pupils *en masse* under the teacher's direction.

Paradoxically, those tasks – regarded, presumably, as 'simplifications' – were distilled from relatively advanced practice and either took for granted or ignored natural starting points for the development of understanding. The twentieth century saw more carefully refined notions of education and the ways in which children learn. For example, the compilers of the 1931 Hadow Report were quite clear that

> A good school ... is not a place of compulsory instruction, but a community of old and young, engaged in learning by co-operative experiment. ... The essential point is that the curriculum should not be loaded with inert ideas and crude blocks of fact. ... It must be vivid, realistic, a stream in motion, not a stagnant pool. (Hadow *et al.* 1931, pp. xvii, xxiii)

Similarly, the 'Butler' Education Act of 1944 recognised the need to educate children according to their 'age, aptitude and ability', and today it is readily acknowledged that not all children learn in the same way. That, together with the increasing variety of curriculum opportunities, suggests at least a tacit acceptance of 'other ways of coming to know'. Yet, notwithstanding the educational developments of the second half of the twentieth century, the corpus of factual knowledge to be *passed on* has retained its primacy not only because correlations of right/wrong and success/failure make it easy to evaluate pupils' progress, but also because there are now more and more demands upon schools to provide evidence of the efficacy of their teaching. Unfortunately, league tables and performance criteria tend to play down the difference between assessment (informed but nevertheless subjective *judgement*) and evaluation (definition of a precise – and, therefore, presumably, indisputable – value). We seem to have reached a point where we accept without question the possibility of *evaluating* all learning in terms which will have the same meaning across the curriculum. As a consequence, we may all too easily allow ourselves to be trapped by compromise, making important what can most easily be evaluated rather than valuing what is important. In which case, why do we bother with 'other ways of coming to know' which, although they may be assessed, cannot be evaluated? – notably, anything that relies upon the exercise of imagination, creative response, and the expression of independent views.

## ■ Music is different

Music has no past; it exists only at the moment when it happens, and no two performances are identical.[2] This is not a disadvantage. On the contrary, it is music's greatest asset because, perhaps more than anything else in our experience, it evokes the essential 'now' without implications of a past and a potential future. Thus, Stravinsky pointed out that only through music are we able to 'realize the present' (1962, p. 53). Musical 'meaning' cannot be separated from the act of presentation. However, the necessity of *present*-ing music – making it present here and now, without which it will not be music at all – does not sit easily with a concept of education that rests mainly upon received factual knowledge and which, by tradition, uses the past to make sense of the present.[3] If we want music to have a role in general education it would seem logical to acknowledge this difference and give prominence to activities that will involve all pupils working directly with music. Yet, in spite of numerous attempts to develop a more *musical* music curriculum for the majority of school pupils, the 'immediacy' of the experience is given scant attention in the classroom, the emphasis being still, as it has been for so long, on pupils absorbing inert information about music.

The reasons for this are not hard to find. Probably very few people would regard music's distinctive 'newness' as a property of the art itself. Doubtless, the majority would see it simply as the most obvious result of musicians performing to audiences. During the middle decades of the twentieth century a new sense of purpose began to be evident in grammar-school music teaching with the development of orchestras, bands, and choirs. The advent of LEA peripatetic instrumental teachers

2 This is true even for concert presentations of electro-acoustic music which consist in the diffusion of works created in a recorded format. The property of 'newness' is evident in the differing circumstances of each presentation (different venues with different acoustic qualities; the changing composition of audiences; make-up of the programmes; etc.).

3 Cf. Quennell 1945, p. 83, on Edward Gibbon's studies in Roman history: for Gibbon '... the past gave to the present the justification that it needed, suggested a continuity in human affairs that, at first glance, seemed often strangely lacking, supplied the perspective essential to a clear and dispassionate view.'

had made it possible for grammar school 'directors of music' to emulate the positive and characteristic features of music in independent schools. Subsequently, the comprehensive schools inherited this practice but, understandably, insisted that the music-making should be seen as part of the curriculum even though rehearsals were normally scheduled 'out-of-timetable'. With rare exceptions, such activities still cater for a minority of pupils – it could hardly be otherwise – but the ultimate justification is that the ensembles *give concerts*. That, in a roundabout way, influenced the programme-note style of timetabled 'music' lessons which, over many years, has subtly emphasised the difference between the concert-giving minority's activity and the musical *in*activity of everyone else. It gave rise to the theory that, although the 'unmusical' majority might not be able to participate in music-making, if their education provided them with enough information about music, they could become 'good listeners'. Have we realised that aim to any greater extent than Trevelyan, 60 years ago, thought we had done with literature? Might it not be more honest to forget the general 'music lessons' and allow music-making to be an option for those who show the appropriate interest and practical talent? Or again, should we not bother at all with music in schools, providing instead dedicated facilities for those who want them in local music schools or conservatoires?

## ■ Words as a substitute for experience

Given the curriculum's focus on factual knowledge it is hardly surprising that there has been so much 'talking about music'. In the memories of some of us who were at school in the 1930s and early 1940s Musical Appreciation may well be associated with Walford Davies's legendary broadcasts (Rainbow, 1989, pp. 294, 309, 346). By contrast, the regular classroom music teaching at secondary level tended to lapse into formula, feeding pupils 'facts' about music often without their hearing any music at all – as, for example, in the teaching of so-called form. As a result, many concert-goers now believe that they must have information before they listen to music. Yet at the same time they may find themselves alienated by what they read! As Bernard Levin famously wrote in an article in *The Times* after attending a performance of Bach's *The Art of Fugue*, and having been thoroughly bemused by the programme-note references to 'fugues by augmentation and diminution' and 'canons *rectus et inversus*': 'The problem with this stuff is that those who can understand it don't need it, and those who need it can't understand it!'

It does seem unfortunate that, in the name of education, people have been brought misguidedly to believe that they need such detail. Originally intended simply as background support, this information is transformed into essential knowledge which, although it may be interesting in itself, has nothing directly to do with what is experienced. Rather, it appears to suggest that, in spite of all the careful artifice of those who labour to create it and present it, *music has to be explained*. People truly believe that they will not appreciate what they hear without words of explanation. And what are they offered? Either a description of what is being 'portrayed', on the assumption that this will give the music some kind of tangibility – even though we all know music cannot 'portray' anything except by association – or else an impenetrable technical analysis plus an account of the composer's life. That kind of information reinforces the conviction that music cannot speak directly to us, which is tantamount to saying that composers and performers don't know what they are doing.

Composers themselves have frequently made it clear that such marginal information is neither helpful nor necessary. For example, Beethoven, in the announcement of his 'Pastoral' symphony, warned listeners that he was not offering them anything so crude as an attempt to imitate the sounds of nature; rather, they should hear it as a 'recollection of feelings'.[4] Debussy, irritated by analysts, remarked, 'You don't capture the mystery of a forest by counting its trees!' – and, on another occasion, 'Insensitive rabble! Can't you listen to chords without demanding to see their identity cards and characteristics? Where have they come from? Where are they

4 See Crowest 1904, pp. 175–6; Kerman & Tyson 1980, p. 383[a]. In his sketches for the symphony Beethoven had noted, 'A recollection of country life ... a matter more of feeling than of painting in sounds' (Forbes 1964, p. 436). In this context the parallel between Beethoven and his exact contemporary Wordsworth is not without interest. The latter, in his 1800 preface to *Lyrical Ballads*, defined poetry as 'the spontaneous overflow of powerful feelings ... [which] takes its origin from emotion recollected in tranquillity' (Wordsworth 1800/1924, p. 246).

going to? Is it really necessary to know this? Just listen. That's enough.' (Boucourechliev 1972, p. 84).[5]

And, of course, he did mean *listen* – that is to say, listen attentively to the progress of the music, immersing yourself in *what happens*. Here are some others:

> What I would like to achieve is music that is self-contained; music determined to free itself from any suggestion of the picturesque; completely non-descriptive and unassociated with any particular locality in space. (Albert Roussel in 1929, cited in Hoérée 1938, p. 66)

> Most people like music because it gives them certain emotions; such as joy, grief, sadness, an image of nature, a subject for day-dreams, or – better still – oblivion from everyday life ... Music would not be worth much if it were reduced to such an end. (Stravinsky 1962, p. 163)

> I believe that every musical work, regardless of the philosophical concepts, emotions and attitudes which may have inspired it, is always 'pure music'. (Szymanowski [1933])

> ... every composer begins with a musical idea – a MUSICAL idea, you understand, not a ... literary or extra-musical idea. (Copland 1957, p. 23)

> I write music so that people can follow, from bar to bar; and know that some notes follow and others don't. (Alexander Goehr, in a broadcast talk introducing a new work)

> If you've gotta ask, you'll never know! (Louis Armstrong when asked to define jazz)

Again, if composers themselves doubt that music can be 'explained', should we be devoting precious school time to providing mere information?

---

5 'Foule ahurie! N'êtes-vous capable d'écouter des accords sans demander à voir leurs cartes d'identité et leurs caractéristiques? D'où viennent-ils? Où vont-ils? Faut-il absolument le savoir? Écoutez. Çela suffit.'

## ■ Making the most of our musical nature

If music is to make a worthwhile contribution to general education we must look beyond its potential for sentimental association; beyond historical and technical information; beyond cultural, sociological or political reference. None of these things truly explains music, for, even without them, music itself is a form of knowledge; not of the same kind as (say) historical or scientific knowledge, and only tenuously connected with the observable, measurable world we call 'reality', but an important 'way of knowing', nevertheless. The very existence of music in our lives is evidence of something we cannot afford to ignore; how otherwise would it have persisted as such a powerful and necessary element in every human society? As Curt Sachs (1944, pp. 21–2) pointed out:

> However far back we trace mankind, we fail to see the springing up of music. Even the most primitive tribes are musically beyond the first attempts. ... [Music] has little to do with the mutable surface of life, and nothing [to do with] the struggle for existence. This is why music is one of the steadiest elements in the evolution of mankind.

Since the invention of sound recording the number of people who are consumers of, rather than participants in, music must have increased enormously, but although those we regard as 'musical' may now be in a minority, musical *understanding* still belongs quite naturally to us all. John Blacking (1959, p. 8) made the point plainly:

> 'My' society claims that only a limited number of people are musical, and yet it behaves as if all people possessed the basic capacity without which no musical function can exist – the capacity to listen to and distinguish patterns of sound.

This is important because, when we begin to consider why music might have a place in the school curriculum, we must believe that a teacher's commitment is to all the pupils, not only to those with conventional talent. Music may have a role in school life socially but, if it is to be a valuable *curriculum* subject, what is done in the classroom must reach out to every pupil; that is to say, it must exploit natural human musicality.

How, then, is this inherent musicality manifest? Not, I think, in the first instance by listening to music, nor even by learning from someone else how to play on an instrument, but by *making up music*. Across the ages most of the world's music has been made up – invented and performed – by musically untutored people. There are still people like that in every culture, and they are still making music. It may be that most of us have come to think of music as something to be listened to – in the same way that we think of paintings as objects to be *looked at* – yet, in essence, both music and paintings are what human beings *make*: it is the act of making that justifies the art.[6]

Here is something everyone can do, using whatever means are most suitable to the immediate purpose: voices, conventional instruments, 'classroom' instruments, or, indeed, any other ways of making and controlling sounds musically. In schools this idea began to be explored seriously in the mid-1950s and early 1960s,[7] although prior to that – indeed, going back to Jean-Jacques Rousseau in the mid-eighteenth century – composing had been advocated as an essential element in basic musical education.[8] Today numerous recordings from many countries provide abundant evidence of children's intuitive musical creativity.[9]

The principle is simple: to teach from what is offered. Even quite young children will make up spontaneous songs which the teacher can encourage

6 David Hockney talks about 'doing the art'. Similarly Giotto, early in the fourteenth century, described his work thus: 'Da capo a fondo ogni pennellata e comporre' (From beginning to end, every stroke is composition).

7 Cf. Schafer 1965; Self 1967; Dennis 1970; Paynter & Aston 1970, all of whom record work undertaken with children during the 1950s and 1960s. For appraisals of these developments see Metcalfe 1987, pp. 97–118; also Pitts 2000.

8 Cf. Rousseau 1762/1979, p. 149: 'in order to know music well, it does not suffice to transmit it; it is necessary to compose it. The one ought to be learned with the other; otherwise one never knows music well.' (Cf. the first English translation (1763): 'or we shall never be masters of this science'.)

9 British examples include pupils' compositions from the 1970s which can be heard in the films, tape–slide programmes and recordings produced by the Schools Council Project, *Music in the Secondary School Curriculum* (1973–82) and, among more recent examples, those on tapes and CDs issued with the *British Journal of Music Education*. Over forty pieces made by children and young people in Italy can be heard on the tape that accompanies *beQuadro* 66/67 (September 1997). Similar compilations, on tape or CD, have been produced in Japan, Norway, and many other countries.

and receive as what David Holbrook, referring to children's poems, has called 'meant gifts' (1967, p. 8).[10] Coral Davies has described how she regularly invited children to tell her, day by day, about things that mattered to them, or things that were happening around them – and to do the 'telling' by *singing* what they wanted to say (Davies, 1986, 1992). In one such example Mary, aged six, sings about trees in autumn:[11]

> Leaves are falling off the tree,
> turning colours and ... blue –
> When they coming down the tree,
> different colours as well.
> One is purple and one is blue and
> one is green and one is brown and
> ONE IS YELLOW!
> When they're falling down the tree.

What do we learn when we listen to this song? First, that it behaves like a piece of music: it could not conceivably be mistaken for anything else. If that seems obvious it is nevertheless important to remember that the one thing everybody knows about music is that it comes in 'pieces'. Moreover, everyone understands that the word 'piece', applied to music, means not a *bit* of something but rather a *whole* of something, self-contained and experientially complete. Common to every piece is what Immanuel Kant called 'the form of finality' (1790/1928, §§10, 11). Although we may never give that a thought, it is what the mind expects and what we find satisfying. 'Understanding' a work of art implies perception of a 'common-sense' relationship between the work as a whole and its materials – for example, in music: melodic motifs, harmonic and rhythmic figures, timbres, varied textures and densities, and so on. Either as listeners to, or as makers of, music, if we are attentive, we shall sense the coherence that is achieved largely by intuitive ways of 'working' the materials *together* – hence the notion of 'com-position': positing or 'putting-in-place-together'

---

10 'The least piece of writing, if the teacher has established the context for proper "giving", will be a "meant" gift.'

11 Track 20 of the tape accompanying *British Journal of Music Education* 9.3 (November 1992).

the invented materials so that expectations emerge and are fulfilled or postponed and brought to ultimate closure in a way which says, '*That's* how it should be: *that* makes sense.'

In six-year-old Mary's spontaneous song about the falling leaves we can hear how she works the materials towards a particular point. In spite of her hesitation before singing 'blue' at the end of the second line, it is clear that she feels the rhythmic pattern of 'turning colours and *blue*' because she reinforces it with the phrase '*different* colours as *well*'. The manner and impetus of that rhythmic reinforcement continues in 'one is purple and *one* is blue and ...', so that the thought flows on with even greater vigour in a larger pattern combining the two short phrases ('one is purple and one is blue and one is green and one is brown and ...'), all of which leads to the singular 'ONE IS YELLOW!' Here is an obvious climax, but that effect is not achieved solely by the powerful high and *fortissimo* delivery. Rather it is the musical thinking-through that ensures that we receive the full impact of this moment.[12] The process begins with 'one is brown'. That is truly the song's crucial point because everything else takes off from there; and, as it does, we realise how all that has gone before now makes even more musical common sense. Having reached this point, the possibility of an ultimately satisfying wholeness becomes apparent. It is the power of the passage from 'one is brown' to 'one is yellow' that gives to the contrastingly gentle phrase that follows ('When they're falling down the tree') a finality of closure that seems both inevitable and 'right'.

It would not be necessary to explain to this child what she has achieved, even if one could think of a way of doing so. What matters is that she has been encouraged to create a musical event which has been received with interest and enthusiasm by the teacher. Simply by making this song, Mary has discovered things that she could not have learned in any other way. It might be said that she is following well-tried and deeply rooted patterns; after all, she is six years old and no doubt she has already heard a lot of music which works more or less in the same way as her song. But she is not singing a song she already knows or has been taught, one made

---

12 Similar to the process that produces a climax in a discussion or a presentation, and that has been characterised as 'thought occupied with indicators of what is common in the passage from one attitude to another'.

up by someone else; this is her invention, words and music. She has made the shape of the song 'her own' and has related that to words which simultaneously generate the melody. Moreover, it seems clear that she understands intuitively the way in which the wholeness of the song – its 'common sense' – depends upon precisely when certain things happen: a precision that is felt, not calculated.

Austin Wright (in Hamilton 1994, p. 142) suggested that a piece of sculpture should be explored

> like a building, a ruin, a landscape, a town. Think how you would cross it, climb it; where you would rest and where you would want to get in the end.

He also described those important intersections as 'the points where things legitimately hang together': moments, so to speak, of achievement which 'add up' and validate the piece by giving it an overall logic. This, too, is how music works. Changes of direction, unexpected extensions and additions, moments when we feel something important happens: all are crucial, in the strict sense of the word, because they mark time and, by so doing, create significant proportions within the overall timescale of a piece. It is the proportions that make sense of what happens. Listening to Mary inventing her song, we too can feel instinctively the rightness of the proportions she creates. Her intuitive 'thinking in music' governs the repetition of phrases and words which engineer that repetition. Thus, the cardinal point ('one is brown'), from which the wholeness of the musical event springs, occurs at about nineteen seconds into the song: a pivotal moment in a piece which, in total, lasts for a fraction over thirty-one

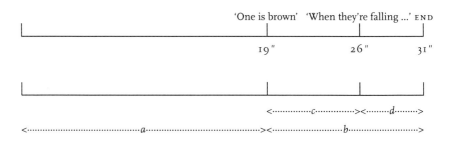

Figure 1  Note: *d* is to *c* as *b* is to *a*.

seconds. Likewise, in the passage from 'one is brown' to the end of the song, the same proportional relationship occurs at 26 seconds, with the start of the closing phrase ('When they're falling down the tree') (see Figure 1).

## ■ Models of perfection

The asymmetrical relationship of one-third to two-thirds in measurements of duration or space has immense significance in the history of the world's poetry, literature, visual arts, architecture and music.[13] We have seen how such relativity occurs naturally in a child's spontaneous song. It is found the world over, in music of every kind, old and new. It is a proportion that is especially satisfying when we observe it in nature – in the shapes and patterning of seashells and fir cones, for example – and, perhaps for this reason, it has been consciously emulated in painting and sculpture. It is discernible in numerous ancient man-made structures and in the 'magic' shapes of the pentagon and five-pointed star. Even in architecture that at first sight seems to be celebrating symmetry, such as Palladian buildings, it is the vertical asymmetry in the positioning of horizontal features, such as string courses, that fascinates and delights the eye. In poetry, as in music, it is again a matter of durations and rhythmic units. The sonnet, for example, makes its most telling division with great subtlety somewhere between the eighth and ninth lines – where it frequently marks a new departure or a striking development of the poem's idea. For the same reason, the iambic pentameter intrigues and satisfies us with its merest hint of emphasis approximately two-thirds of the way through each line.[14]

'There is no excellent beauty that hath not some strangeness in the proportion', wrote Francis Bacon (1612/1825, p. 145); and, indeed, it would appear that the human mind does find greater satisfaction in asymmetry

---

13  The precise point in space or moment in time – the so-called 'Golden Section' – is the product of $n \times 0.618$ (where $n$ is length or duration). The Fibonacci sequence expresses the same relationship (1, 2, 3, 5, 8, 13, 21, etc.).

14  I am indebted to Mr R. T. Jones, formerly Senior Lecturer in the Department of English and Related Literature in the University of York, for pointing out so concisely that, of all the rhythmic patterns in the English language, 'It is the one we like to hear the most, / And we can also *speak* it if we try.'

than it does in symmetry. Perhaps this is because, compared with the somewhat static properties of 'binary' symmetry, the Trinitarian dynamics of asymmetry – acculturation/realisation/revelation – lead the brain, via eye or ear, most powerfully to a sensation of wellbeing and *wholeness*. Our hope is evident in that word: to be kept inviolate in spite of the worst that life can do to us. Thus, to be whole is to be hale, is to be healed, is to be holy – the realisation of the quality that, however we express it, makes us truly *human* beings.

Obviously, the processes of thinking and making that we now call 'art' go far back into the origins of humanity. The medium is indeed the message, and the characteristic 'making sense in its own terms' – that necessary feature of every art object or event – is surely a response to those things which, because we cannot take hold of them, ultimately trouble us most: time and space, and their mysterious relationship with life and death. Even in our modern world we confront and accommodate these problems by making models of perfection – although we may neither recognise them as such, nor be willing to acknowledge that that is what we are doing. Our predecessors constructed temples and cathedrals to make space graspable; we build skyscrapers and geodesic domes. We also, of course, continue to make sculptures and paintings, and, notwithstanding the 'subject', an artist's primary concern will always be the careful handling of scale and proportion to offer glimpses of perfected space. Likewise, in poetry and literature we are conscious of a similar *pacing* of the thought to fulfil ideas in forms which themselves, in addition to their literary substance, give satisfaction and make sense. Of all mankind's attempts to model perfection, music is, perhaps, the most subtle. Its meaning is manifest not in objects viewed or touched but in *events* that can only be experienced in the time it takes to make each one audible. Music lifts off from the surface of life: it cannot be concerned with depiction or description of worldly reality, even though its points of departure are frequently found there.

This should not prevent us from using music in whatever ways we choose, worldly or otherwise! We can make it mean whatever we want it to mean – and undoubtedly it does inspire an infinite number of different uses and interpretations; but that is possible only because, at root, *music means the same thing to everyone*. Whatever the overlay of cultural or sentimental reference, stylistic decoration or technical virtuosity, what finally convinces anyone that a piece 'succeeds' is the music itself. That is achieved not by what other people write or say about it, but through our experience of, and perception of, structural proportions in the piece *as it progresses*. The longer, more extensive sections are assimilated first, the mind establishing the relationship between idea and materials. That brings realisation. Now it is clear what is happening, but there is more to come; and often this can be surprising, particularly as we approach the ultimate point of closure. The moment of revelation which puts the seal of finality on a work must not be too long delayed, nor should it appear too soon: hence the shorter section, related to the first in a proportion we recognise intuitively.

Walter Pater believed that 'All art constantly aspires towards the condition of music'; to that state in which 'the end is not distinct from the means, the form from the matter, the subject from the expression' (Pater, 1873/1912, pp. 135, 139). It could, however, be argued that rather than merely aspiring to that end, all the arts do, in fact, achieve it. For some, the means of expression – language, visual forms and images – may seem to be tied to mundane existence; yet all, like music, are concerned with perceptions of proportion and completeness which suggest an 'other' reality. In the strict meaning of the word, art 'entertains' us, in that its principal function is to 'hold [us] between' (*inter tenere*) two levels of experience, two kinds of reality. Thus, music operates in virtual (psychological) time, although we are aware of it taking place in 'real' (chronometric) time.[15] A similar perception of the precise points at which significant things happen in time or space applies in our appreciation of every art form.

## ■ A place for music in the school curriculum

Schools today have to fulfil a variety of needs, social as well as educational, but the core of their responsibility is, as it always has been, the learning that takes place under the guidance of teachers in classrooms. That core is increasingly under pressure, not only from the demands of testing

---

15  For example, all those present at a concert could agree on the time when a piece began and the time when it stopped, but everyone would have a different impression of how the time passed during the course of the piece.

and appraisal but also from expansion – for example, 'literacy' hours and the reintroduction of 'citizenship' lessons. We ought to be sure that everything we put into the curriculum has educational justification. Time was when we were content to accept music as a relaxation from the rigours of seemingly more demanding subjects! That was not good enough then, and it won't do now. Neither will it suffice to impose on music a spurious academicism to make it appear rigorous in exactly the same terms as some other curriculum subjects. Apart from anything else, that is unnecessary: music has its own rigour in the demands of sensitivity, imagination, and inventiveness common to all artistic endeavour – qualities which are sorely needed in the modern world. This, I suggest, is what we should expect, first and foremost, from musical education in the classroom – an education accessible to all pupils. The justification for music in these circumstances is not more information to be assimilated, but a very important human quality to be exercised and developed: the potential we all have to make art by making up music. There could be no better illustration of the old maxim 'You cannot teach anyone anything she or he does not already know.' It calls to mind Herbert Read's often quoted words: 'Appreciation is not acquired by passive contemplation: we only appreciate beauty on the basis of our own creative aspirations' (1958, p. 298).

Composition – I prefer to call it 'making up music' – is the most natural thing in the world. The only stimulus it requires is the opportunity and encouragement to do it. It is quite simply through 'doing the art' that not only do we learn about the nature of music itself – thereby achieving understanding of what more experienced musicians have been able to do – but also we use and develop, in many subtle ways, our powers of judgement, the confidence to take decisions, and the courage to stand by those decisions. Up to now, the principal hurdle has been music teachers' lack of experience in composing, perhaps because of an emphasis, in their training, on performance skills. By contrast we would be hard pressed to think of art teachers we have known who were not active in their own right as creative artists.

The first thing is to develop the right atmosphere: one in which it is assumed that what students do in music lessons is to make up pieces, present them, and discuss them. At least in the early stages, such pieces will not be notated. Like the bulk of the world's music they will be invented directly through experiment and improvisation, confirmed by repetition, and remembered. This is as it should be because it places the emphasis on what is heard rather than what is seen on paper. For the teacher, the essential quality is an ability to comment purposefully and encouragingly on pieces pupils produce, either in small groups or individually. The teacher's observations must follow on immediately from the presentation of the music, drawing in all other members of the class in addition to the composers themselves to recall what happened in the piece: the relationship of materials to idea, and the extent to which the idea was fulfilled – that is to say, 'fully filled out'. Much of this will be achieved through appropriate questioning, with occasional reference, preferably by demonstration, to compositions by other composers who have explored similar ideas. These teaching techniques have been extensively documented over the past thirty-five years, but still many teachers lack confidence, not only in their own ability but also in students' potential to respond. The tendency to revert to instruction is understandable. Collaboration with other arts teachers could be helpful. Apart from the constraints of time, this need not preclude other aspects of musical education, either in the classroom or in out-of-timetable activities such as choirs and orchestras. In general, music in schools would benefit by closer association with the other creative arts and with those things that underpin their place in the curriculum – the age-old natural processes of 'thinking and making' which manifestly produce such worthwhile results in the visual arts, creative writing, dance, and drama. Only on that basis shall we ever realise a school music curriculum which really can involve everyone and justify the time we give to it.

## ■ References

Ascham, R. 1570/1927. 'The First Booke for the Youth'. In *The Scholemaster*. Ed. E. Arber. London: Constable & Co.

Bacon, F. 1612/1825. *Essays or Counsels Civil and Moral, XLIII: Of Beauty*. In *Lord Bacon's Works*, vol. 1. London: William Richardson.

Blacking, J. 1959. *How Musical is Man?* Washington, DC: University of Washington Press.

Boucourechliev, A. 1972. *Debussy: la révolution subtile*. Paris: Fayard.

Copland, A. 1957. *What to Listen for in Music*. New York: McGraw-Hill.

Crowest, F. J. 1904. *Beethoven*. London: J. M. Dent.

Davies, C. 1986. 'Say it till a Song Comes: Reflections on Songs Invented by Children 3–13.' *British Journal of Music Education* 3.3, pp. 279–93.

Davies, C. 1992. 'Listen to My Song: A Study of Songs Invented by Children Aged 5 to 7 Years.' *British Journal of Music Education* 9.1, pp. 19–48.

Dennis, B. 1970. *Experimental Music in Schools*. Oxford: Oxford University Press.

Forbes, E. (ed.) 1964. *Thayer's Life of Beethoven*. Princeton, NJ: Princeton University Press.

Hadow, Sir W. H., *et al.* 1931. 'Report of the Consultative Committee on the Primary School.' London: HMSO.

Hamilton, J. 1994. *The Sculpture of Austin Wright*. London: The Henry Moore Foundation, in association with Lund Humphries Ltd.

Hoérée, A. 1938. *Albert Roussel*. Paris, n.p.

Holbrook, D. 1967. *Children's Writing*. Cambridge: Cambridge University Press.

Kant, I. 1790/1928. *The Critique of Teleological Judgement*. Trans. J. C. Meredith. Oxford: Clarendon Press.

Kendall, S. 1986. 'The Harmony of Human Life: An Exploration of the Ideas of Pestalozzi and Froebel in Relation to Music Education.' *British Journal of Music Education* 3.1, pp. 35–48.

Kerman, J., and A. Tyson 1980. 'Beethoven.' In *The New Grove Dictionary of Music and Musicians*. Ed. S. Sadie. Vol. 2. London: Macmillan.

Metcalfe, M. 1987. 'Towards the Condition of Music: The Emergent Aesthetic of Music Education.' In *Living Powers*. Ed. P. Abbs. London: Falmer Press.

Pater, W. 1873/1912. *The Renaissance: Studies in Art and Poetry*. London: Macmillan.

Paynter, J., and P. Aston 1970. *Sound and Silence*. Cambridge: Cambridge University Press.

Pitts, S. 2000. *A Century of Change in Music Education*. Aldershot: Ashgate.

Quennell, P. 1945. 'Edward Gibbon'. In *Four Portraits*. London: Collins.

Rainbow, B. 1989. *Music in Educational Thought and Practice*. Aberystwyth: Boethius Press; 2nd edition enlarged with further chapters by Gordon Cox, a foreword from Sir Peter Maxwell Davies, and a biographical introduction by Peter Dickinson. Woodbridge: Boydell Press, 2006.

Read, H. 1958. *Education through Art.* London: Faber & Faber.

Rousseau, J.-J. 1762/1979. *Émile, or, On Education.* Trans. A. Bloom. New York: Basic Books.

Sachs, C. 1944. *The Rise of Music in the Ancient World: East and West.* London: Dent.

Schafer, R. M. 1965. *The Composer in the Classroom.* Don Mills, ON: BMI Canada.

Self, G. 1967. *New Sounds in Class.* London: Universal Edition.

Skinner, B. F. 1964. 'New Methods and New Aims in Teaching.' *New Scientist* 22, no. 392, pp. 483–4.

Skinner, B. F. 1968. *The Technology of Teaching.* New York: Meredith Corporation.

Stravinsky, I. 1962. *An Autobiography.* New York: W. W. Norton.

Trevelyan, G. 1942. *English Social History: A Survey of Six Centuries: Chaucer to Queen Victoria.* London: Longmans, Green & Co.

Wordsworth, W. 1800/1924. 'Preface to *Lyrical Ballads.*' In W. Wordsworth and S. T. Coleridge. *Lyrical Ballads.* Ed. H. Littledale. London: Oxford University Press.

*Fourth Bernarr Rainbow Lecture, given at Trinity College of Music, Greenwich, 19 October 2004*

# A Provocative Perspective on Music Education Today

## JOHN STEPHENS

John Stephens, OBE, has had a long career in music education as teacher, adviser, inspector, lecturer and examiner. He taught in Portsmouth and Harlow, Essex, and was County Music Adviser for Shropshire. He was appointed to HM Inspectorate in 1968 with an assignment in counties across southern England, and Assessor to the Schools Council Project *Music in the Secondary Curriculum*, directed by Professor John Paynter. Then, in 1976, he became Staff Inspector of Music in the Inner London Education Authority, where he pioneered the bringing together of teachers and professional musicians and widened music provision. Finally he was Head of Education at Trinity College of Music and was appointed OBE in 1998.

HALF A CENTURY AGO THIS YEAR I first stood in front of a class of secondary-school pupils as their music master, without a hint of imagining that I might one day have the honour to be invited to give a lecture in the name of a distinguished and much-respected music educator of the time, Bernarr Rainbow. I humbly offer this perspective on music education today to honour him and the countless practitioners and thinkers who have, over the years, influenced my own career and who continue to shape the future course of music education.

The provocation suggested by the title is intended to be stimulating and suggestive, even perhaps outrageous, rather than an alternative provocation which my dictionary defines as 'irritating, irksome and exasperating'. I am indebted to Peter Renshaw and Peter Dickinson, who commented on early drafts of this paper, and to many others who have contributed to my thinking. However, the perspective in the title is entirely my own and I accept responsibility, and ask your indulgence for my prejudice, bias and shortcomings.

## ■ Roles

To provide an element of coherence for this perspective I wish to focus upon 'roles' in music education and I invite you for a moment to consider some of the activities undertaken by those whose vocation is to educate others, from toddlers to totterers. Education is, of course, a life-spanning process which is not restricted by age or confined by the institutions we call schools, colleges and universities.

Clearly in formal education teachers play a central role, but others, including professional musicians, performers, composers, and that relatively recent phenomenon the animateur, have contributory and supporting roles. So too do politicians and administrators who often have key strategic, decision-making functions which affect the direction of both formal and informal music education.

It was Roy Shaw who, as Secretary-General of the Arts Council in the early 1980s, secured the formal links between arts organisations and the education world through the appointment of its first education officer. Subsequently this spawned education officers and departments in most of today's professional music organisations. And it was Chris Smith, as Secretary of State for Culture Media and Sport, who, in 1998, had the vision to create Youth Music to provide lottery funds to encourage young people's music-making outside the formal school setting, and to influence musical activity in the wider community. Both initiatives have had a profound influence upon those who, in many different ways, play a role in today's music education.

The term 'role' is frequently employed in social psychology to denote a set of expectations associated with a particular position. David Hargreaves,[1] my former colleague in the Inner London Education Authority (ILEA), sees 'role' as a reference to prescriptions as well as expectations about the behaviour of a person occupying a given position. Thus we expect an outcome of teaching to be that pupils or students learn, and an outcome of conducting that a satisfactory performance follows the rehearsal: two roles to which I shall return later.

1 David H. Hargreaves, *Interpersonal Relations and Education* (London: Routledge & Kegan Paul, 1972).

## ■ Complementary roles

Many role positions have 'complementary roles' with which the principal position is linked: teachers have pupils, conductors have orchestras, politicians have electors, composers have performers who in turn have audiences. Fulfilling a role depends on the willingness of the complementary player to share in the relationship.

This is relatively straightforward until we examine the complexities of the many layers of expectations which bear upon the enterprise of music education. Parents have expectations of schools and students have expectations of universities and colleges. Expectations change and vary according to the educational and political environment of the day. The introduction of student-fees in a consumer-economy education market will place them in a new relationship with their university or college. As their hard-earned cash meets much of the tuition costs previously met by a remote, unseen public-funding body, their expectations of their courses of study and the resources provided for them will have a sharper focus.

Politicians articulate expectations as they seek to implant their own ideologies on educational institutions in an attempt to demonstrate how effectively they control public resources to serve their particular philosophy. A standardised curriculum for schools and for teacher training, attainment tests, league tables and targets are examples of mechanisms used by administrations to play a controlling role in 'education, education, education'.

There are many varied interests that bring a set of expectations and fulfil a role in the process of music education. For some, the compelling drive and commitment cements them into a host of organisations for professional debate and exchange, and the promotion of methods: a federation for this, a society, council or forum for that, and an association for something else. My one-time HMI colleague and mentor Raymond Roberts once declared that it would not surprise him to see the formation of a society for the preservation of F sharp.

Professional arts organisations, including orchestras and opera companies, offer schools educational projects with musicians undertaking a quasi-teaching role. Visiting instrumental teachers provide, for a variable proportion of pupils, specialist tuition on a whole range of instruments.

All contribute in various ways to musical education. Perhaps only in the conservatoires, universities and private-teaching studios is the exclusive one-to-one role of the specialist music teacher uncomplicated by many supplementary roles.

As politicians are lobbied over concerns that 'we are in danger of losing the UK's pole global position to countries who offer better musical opportunities',[2] we see eminent musicians who understand and keep up to date with issues in music education stepping outside a performing role to use their musical authority in an attempt to influence government policy. The list of professional champions of music education far outstrips that for other disciplines such as drama, visual arts or dance.

Politicians write music manifestos which barely clothe their political ideologies and mask deficiencies in public funding. 'Music is magic' is the opening statement of the most recent government manifesto, which fails to produce a rabbit, and leaves the hat for begging.[3] A warmly platitudinous document, it fails to address even the most basic of issues, such as the inequalities and unevenness in the provision for music education throughout the country, and the vexed issue of who will pay for instrumental teaching in schools – local authorities, national government or parents.

Politicians, professional musicians, voluntary bodies promoting this and that: all roles are multi-dimensional, complex, fluid, and even at times contradictory.

## ■ Context

In this perspective of music education today I shall identify three roles which have significance in influencing the direction of music education, which is not a fixed notion firmly established within a rigid framework. Teachers of my youth were content to teach from the *National Song Book* and *Songs from Around the World*, with wind-up gramophone servicing

---

2 E. Glennie, 'Renaissance of Music Education?', *ISM Music Journal* 71.4 (September 2004).

3 Department for Education and Skills, *The Music Manifesto: More Music for More People* (Annesley: DfES Publications, 2004), unpaginated.

appreciation lessons which flew the flag of heritage from the high moral ground. Globalisation and technology have brought us world music, gamelan, computers, electronic and synthesised sounds in which the vernacular also jostles for a place. The context within which today's teachers make judgements and choices is far more complex than they were half a century ago.

The three roles which I identify are those of leader, partner and supporter. This is not a random selection, but represents essential and distinctive components for cultural development in our society. I believe that a closer examination of these roles reveals weaknesses in current structures in education, including the way we attempt to train teachers of music; how musical talent, in whatever genre or form it may appear, is nurtured and developed; and how resources of public funding for music education are presently deployed.

Hopefully, we can also celebrate the achievements of those individuals who, often against all the odds, have exploited their roles to make something worthwhile happen. Thinking about roles will also enhance our appreciation of the potential within our own individual spheres of influence, whether teacher or tutor, lecturer or listener, researcher or repetiteur, conductor or coach, or any of the eighty or so more descriptions of roles identified in Youth Music's report *Creating a Land with Music*.[4]

## ■ Leader

In giving prominence to the role of leader I wish to underscore my belief that the quality of leadership in music education will determine future outcomes. Future generations need musical leaders. I believe that we currently need them in informal as well as formal settings.

Leader is a term familiar in the orchestral world, with specific functions which have a direct bearing upon the quality and efficiency of rehearsal and performance. The leader operates from a position of technical and musical authority, anticipating, negotiating, instructing, even directing, in

4 Rick Rogers, *Creating a Land with Music: The Work, Education and Training of Musicians in the 21st Century* (London: Higher Education Funding Council for England, 2002).

a role which weaves alongside that of the conductor as the warp and weft of a fabric.

I am going to explore four leadership roles: in musical leadership those associated with performing and conducting, and in pedagogic leadership the roles of teacher and animateur.

### □ Music Leader

We may use the term 'taking the lead' in a jazz ensemble, or 'lead guitar', 'lead singer' in popular music, denoting the musical prominence given to a solo performer in which the skills of improvisation and invention are likely to be prominent alongside executant proficiency. Within the flow of jazz and chamber music, roles of leadership are exchanged through a series of stylistic conventions, physical gestures and signals. Such moments provide often exciting insights into the character of the performer who, quite literally, leads us through the music as a guide might introduce us to some unfamiliar architecture, exhibition or gallery. Good leaders are guides, pied pipers in the best sense.

Musical leadership is exercised through the medium of musical expression; verbal explanation and justification are unnecessary. Further, it is not restricted to a single genre or form of music-making: it is an essential component for the amateur as for the professional, for the music classroom as for the concert hall. The first requirement of a good music teacher is to be a good leader.

Qualities of leadership are demonstrated through performance and, notably in the orchestral world, the skill to achieve blend, balance and coherence in ensemble without the extrovert qualities of a soloist – akin to the Chinese proverb which reminds us that there is tacit leadership by saying: 'When we arrived, we asked "who led us here?"'.

The conductor provides another model of leadership, which in a directing mode superficially appears to be didactic, non-democratic and totalitarian in applying judgements. Behind and beyond this are the subtleties of the roles of enabler, facilitator and encourager, stamped with the imprint of the conductor's own interpretation and personality. Defining these characteristics assists us in exploring the differences as well as the similarities between the leadership roles of a musician and a music teacher.

To help distinguish between the roles of conductor and teacher, we might pose the question: 'What is the difference between a rehearsal and a music lesson?' From an initial observation we might conclude that the skills required are similar – those elements which are found in the syllabuses of many music colleges as transferable skills. But observe closely, as I have on countless occasions. During the rehearsal a conductor might, for a period, isolate one group, section, or even individual performer. Ignoring all others in the ensemble, the focus is on the selected group. When the skilful music teacher listens in the classroom to a composition devised by a group of pupils, the rest of the class is given a task: Tell me what you hear. What features of this please you? What is the structure of the piece? All pupils are task-oriented. Of course the unskilled teacher adopts the conductor's mode and ignores the rest of the class. Both the conductor and the teacher build upon the previous experiences of their orchestra or their class.

A colleague and former chief executive of the London Philharmonic Orchestra told me of an internationally renowned conductor rehearsing the orchestra at Glyndebourne, spending a whole session on half of a Mozart overture in the knowledge that the players would 'transfer' to the rest of the opera his stylistic and interpretive requirements. Such differences define the respective role of conductor and teacher, and identify the distinctive range of skills required for each.

My example is, of course, selective. However, close observation of lessons and rehearsals provide further distinctions between the conductor and the teacher. The skills of musical leadership and pedagogic leadership may be complementary, even at times overlapping. However, there are significant differences and, even for the intuitive musician and the intuitive teacher, these require specific development. It should not be assumed that the performing musician or the musical director has the leadership skills to fulfil the role of teacher or lecturer. I have observed too many make the attempt and fail. Musicians who are mindful of the skills of their own profession can learn much from skilled practitioners in teaching.

Until fairly recently our conservatoire system of music education was built on the premise that a high level of performance skill was all that was required to train emerging talent. It is quite clearly not so, as was confirmed to me when, invited by the then principal of a music college to visit classes in teaching and pedagogic studies, I reported that he ran a music hotel: lecturers booked rooms, gave lessons and disappeared. Calling themselves professors, they were distinguished and revered in performance while lacking almost any skill in fulfilling a teaching role. That was nearly fifteen years ago. Progress towards establishing objective criteria for the skills required to teach in higher education has been slow. Too many who presently teach in premium-funded institutions merely replicate the role-models of their own teachers. Such levels of unqualified and unconfirmed competence would not be tolerated in industry.

The amateur teacher, like the amateur surgeon, is simply contradictory. Whilst music-making for the amateur can be a highly satisfying experience, uncluttered by many of the expectations of the professional, in teaching there is simply no room for the amateur.

## □ Teacher

Having enjoyed the privilege during my professional career of observing many thousands of teachers in their classrooms, studios and lecture halls, I have always been impressed by the creative capacity of the skilled teacher to encourage, stimulate, motivate, promote, direct, inspire and diagnose the moments when the young mind is fertile for learning. Whilst effective teachers draw upon a range of pedagogic skills, including planning the learning process, diagnosing its development and assessing progress, they all bring to their role an individual flavour which defines each teacher as different from the next.

To illustrate a specific pedagogic skill, let us consider the ability to frame and ask the right question. Questioning technique is, in my view, critical in fulfilling the role of a teacher, who deploys it to arouse interest, challenge, and stimulate the imagination. What is its relative minor? – assesses factual knowledge. In which composition do you hear this motif? – evaluates aural skills. How are you intending to finger this passage? – monitors technical understanding. How do you do this? – facilitates reflective practice. How can you achieve that? – poses a challenge. What would happen if? – opens creative possibilities.

Such questions do not come randomly to the skilled teacher, neither are they satisfied by an answer from a single pupil in a class or student in a lecture – regrettably often the hallmark of an inexperienced musician trying to undertake the role of teacher. No, the skilled teacher will know how to elaborate responses and promote learning from those in the class who may not have responded with an answer. Do you and you agree with the answer? What do you think? How can we see if this answer works? Can you think of another way of solving this problem?

Developing these skills and many others necessary for effective and efficient teaching is part of the process of learning to be a teacher. Today there are many routes into gaining a professional qualification in teaching, including that which gives Qualified Teacher Status (QTS). This process has always incorporated some direct experience and training in the classroom. Over the years there has been a shift of emphasis in the supervision of this aspect of the training, now called 'school experience' rather than 'school practice', from college lecturers to school teachers. Whilst I believe that it is absolutely right that current practitioners should assume a key role in training aspiring teachers, a clear distinction needs to be made between their functions of educating the pupils in the school and training the student teachers. The two are not incompatible, but the distinction needs to be made.

My experience of external examining in teacher training establishments leads me to conclude that many teachers become so focused on their teacher–pupil role that they overlook their mentoring role in training their future colleagues who, during their period of school experience in some schools, become an additional member of staff with little guidance in pedagogic skills or reflective practices. Visiting a school with a distinguished lecturer who had a lifetime's experience in training teachers, I was amazed that she had to ask permission of the school to join me in observing a student-teacher. Her penetrating comments at the conclusion of the session showed that she knew far more about training aspiring teachers than anyone in the school. As structures change there is a temptation to overlook the value of past experience.

A healthy environment for trainee teachers requires thriving music activities which offer good models and clear guidance. The current system relies upon schools sustaining sufficient high-quality models in which to train the next generation of teachers. We are told by the 2002–3 annual report of HM Chief Inspector of Schools that over 40 per cent of schools under-perform in the quality of their music provision.[5] One of the report's key requirements in music education nationally is to improve leadership and management of music. The Teacher Training Agency statistics show regional variations in recruiting students for allocated places to train as a secondary school music teacher. The under-recruitment by nearly one third in the West Midlands must be a concern where the majority of students train in the area then proceed to teach in a West Midlands school. This continuing shortfall in new music teachers compounds the matter of the quality of leadership.

## □ *Animateur*

Professional musicians have, for decades, worked closely with schools, and their association with the education process has had numerous benefits for both professions. Robert Mayer organised children's concerts by professional orchestras. Simon Rattle vigorously challenged the politicians of the day when, in 1990, they wanted to remove practical elements of the National Curriculum for music. Composer Peter Maxwell Davies, who in the 1960s was music master at Cirencester Grammar School, is a champion for school music.[6] Richard McNicol, followed by Gillian Moore, were the first animateurs, taking professional musicians into schools, not to teach, but to lead pupils and their teachers in the discovery of music.

The Inner London Education Authority, before it was politically dismembered, supported numerous initiatives for its pupils to attend professional musical events in the capital, not by the second team playing for a schools' matinée, but by international artists who frequently met the pupils during an interval or volunteered to call by a school during their London stay. These included composers such as Tippett, one-time head of music at Morley College, and Lutosławski, and conductors such as Charles Mackerras, Andrew Davis, Mark Elder and more. Musicians from India brought tablas and sitars to perform their music in London schools. Other

---

5 OFSTED/TSO, 'Annual Report of HM Inspector of Schools (2002–3)'.

6 See his Royal Philharmonic Society Lecture, p. 99 below.

musicians came from China, South America, and the farthest corners of the globe. As the capital welcomed those from overseas who brought their families and made their homes here, so professional musicians of these cultural traditions followed. The pattern was not restricted to London, but was replicated in urban areas across the country.

How was this relationship between the worlds of professional music and education fostered and developed? It happened through the resources of local education authorities and the leadership of their music advisers, inspectors and advisory teachers. They initiated all of these exciting programmes and activities, unaffordable for an individual school, which benefitted all of the schools in their authority. Music advisers of the day recognised that to develop a stronger relationship between artists and teachers, as the Arts Council wished to encourage, musicians should remove the barriers of the concert platform and proscenium stage to work with teachers in their schools. Animateurs skilfully facilitated this process.

The animateur's role was forged by music advisers who had direct responsibility for the strategic development of the whole range of musical activities in youth and adult education as well as schools. The strategic function of local authority music advisers, originally called music organisers and initially funded by the generosity of the Carnegie Foundation, placed them in a position of being able to support the new role of animateur – it might be said that they created it. Increasing central government control, weakening of the influence of local education authorities, along with devolved funding to individual schools, have all contributed to the demise of the direct influence and strategic role of music advisers whose work covered informal as well as formal education. Some who previously had distinguished careers in musical leadership and influence – well beyond that of present-day music services – now find themselves sitting in classrooms ticking Office for Standards in Education inspection boxes.

'Aminateur' is not a comfortable word, but it does convey the right sense of movement, making something happen, a mover and possibly a shaker. Rick Rogers in the text for his *Routes into Teaching Music* recognises the role many musicians wish to fulfil within a learning environment whilst not seeking to become fully qualified teachers in a school or college. He cites the music animateur as 'another way to describe musicians who work as leaders and facilitators. An animateur is a practising musician who uses his or her skills, talents and personality, to enable others to compose, create, perform or engage with music'.[7] Through their experience and skill in the music profession they bring to the learning enterprise a dimension which is outside that of the teacher. They work in hospitals and prisons, village halls and community centres as well as schools and colleges. Their role does not have the permanence of a teacher and it is often directed towards a specific objective such as a performance or, because that implies too rigid a framework, 'a sharing' or 'work in progress'. Whilst many are driven by artistic goals, some have an agenda which addresses more utilitarian ends, placing an emphasis on the social or therapeutic value of their work. For these animateurs, self-expression takes priority over artistic merit, technical accomplishment and progression in learning. Often the outcomes are musically shallow projects seldom related to repertoire.

The language which animateurs use to describe their work indicates how they see their role. Workshops and projects are their frame of reference whilst the teacher operates within terms like lesson, curriculum and assessments. For the teacher, extrinsic outcomes – such as marks, grades and examinations – take priority over the artistically driven animateurs, who see an intrinsic value in the musical activity itself.

Formal contexts such as schools and colleges provide structures for different role-models; there are rules and regulations, a hierarchy of authority, and what might be viewed as captive audiences within which the school-based animateur can operate. Similar structures rarely exist in the informal sector which drives animateurs working in this field into the classification of 'community musician', a soft, left-wing and meaningless term. The very heart of musical activity is in communication with others: all musicians are community musicians.

What then is the complementary role to the animateur? As conductors have orchestras, politicians have electors, and teachers have pupils, I conclude that animateurs have musicians as their role partners. They expect those of all ages with whom they work, irrespective of the levels of

---

7 Rick Rogers, *Routes into Teaching Music: A Guide for Every Kind of Musician about how to Train and Work as a Teacher of Music* (Annesley: DfES Publications, 2004), p. 76.

musical skills, to behave as musicians. The integrity of the musical process is at the heart of their mission.

## ■ Partner

We have seen how significant the role-partner is in exploring qualities of leadership, and I hope it will offer a further perspective to consider some notions of partnership. The strong partnerships that exist in music education greatly enrich the whole operation and benefit pupils and students. Specialist peripatetic teachers go from school to school, partnering the resident music teacher in delivering the curriculum. Professional musicians are also frequent partners in the same enterprise. Governments, administrators and parents also claim a partnership role in the education of the young. The nature of these partnerships varies according to the expectations each has of the other and the duration of the partnership.

The violin or guitar teacher who regularly visits a school absorbs its ethos, as well as an understanding of its rules and regulations, the times of lessons, names of pupils and where the coffee machine is located. The regularity of contact provides a perspective which strengthens the partnership. Short-term partnerships, such as those undertaken by an animateur, do not have the same opportunities. A senior Arts Council officer told me that it takes eighteen months to make a secure partnership between artist and school.

It may assist an understanding of partnerships if we briefly consider some models of partnership. Country dance partners twirl round, smile and move on to the next in line. Beyond committing to the dance, there is very little option as to who comes along in an engagement which at best lasts a few bars. This has the virtue of restricting the duration of unwanted partnerships, but curtails the opportunity to extend one which shows promise. Partners may know very little of each other before the encounter and, apart from a comfortable feeling, probably not much afterwards.

Tennis partners, on the other hand, usually exert some choice in selecting a fellow player. They understand each other's strengths and weaknesses, covering for one and exploiting the other; they judge how far their combined efforts can tackle the opposition. During the course of play each anticipates, seizing the initiative or offering support as appropriate. The more that they play in partnership, the greater the opportunity to develop their combined skills and knowledge of their partner's technical capability – a commitment which may provide a basis for future development.

The third model is that of business partnerships. These tend towards a more formal environment with contracts to define responsibilities and expectations. This partnership prospers when each investor is content with the returns from investments. A raft of complementary skills within the enterprise may enhance the outcomes. Here the risks as well as the expectations are assessed.

These models, which in practice overlap and flow into each other, suggest that the term 'partner' can denote a range of different functions. The country-dance model implies a broad coverage through numerous, usually short-term partnerships – the kind of relationship into which many arts organisations are forced by the regulations of project funding. There is little time to make judgements which might prove to have a significant long-term influence. However, business partners will assess the likely duration of a contract to achieve their stated objectives.

The Arts Council and other government agencies, along with numerous benefactors, appear to make frequent reference to the importance of partnerships, implying that it is a good thing to get together, although there is little about how this might work in practice. Are, for example, the Arts Council-funded Creative Partnerships a twirl on the dance floor for itinerant artists, or is there something more fundamental, to do with compatibility, commitment and the time it takes for partnerships to mature and flourish?

The enduring memories left with the children who work with artists in these schemes are wholly worthwhile and may well be of lasting value. Whilst there are often concerns about the legacy – what remains after the completion of an interaction – the significance is rarely measured in terms of the time necessary to establish and nurture a meaningful partnership. The distinction has to be made between performers in the classroom – with captive audiences – and artists who develop an educational partnership.

Where artists and schools come together to work for the benefit of pupils, both need an understanding of their role, along with practical details of how a school operates: its codes and regulations, for example, rules of rewards and sanctions, how progress is defined, monitored and recorded and the duration of attention span for a particular age group.

Partnership is also concerned with 'give and take', and knowing when to give and when to take. It has a dynamic of its own, which varies from partner to partner. Governments also say they fulfil a partnership role as they provide for the regulation and control, along with the statutory framework within which our formal education system operates. The shift from free instrumental tuition, universal throughout my professional career, to a public/private partnership, with parents contributing in some areas as much as 60 per cent of tuition costs, is but one example of the outcome of changing values in society and a shifting emphasis in government policy.

The costs of providing instrumental tuition have always been high, especially where students are taught on a one-to-one basis. Music colleges claim premium funding to meet these costs, a facility not always enjoyed by university music departments who provide individual tuition. In the schools sector music services charge either parents or schools. There is no uniformity: even within a single education authority schools pass on a varying proportion of the costs. Whilst there is a statutory requirement to remit fees for those on various levels of benefit, the variations begin to look like different scales of tickets to travel on a train to Manchester: Savers, Super-Savers, Away-days, APEX, Standard and the like. Musical talent is not restricted to those who can afford to pay.

Whilst the government's Music and Dance scheme goes some way to underwriting support for pupils at the junior conservatoires and in collaboration with Youth Music and national bodies like the National Youth Orchestra, it excludes the talent which is evident outside the Western art tradition. Public funding support to develop and train musical talent is a lottery dependent upon where you live, what your parents earn and what kind of music you choose to study.

The inconsistencies evident in the government *Music Manifesto*, which includes a commitment to 'giving every primary school child opportunities for sustained and progressive tuition offered free of charge or at a reduced rate', goes unnoticed by the signatories.[8] Commitment without cash. Worthy statements of intent, without the backing of increased public funds, are applauded whilst the key partners in the enterprise – the parents – are ignored.

When, in 1997, the government rescued music services with a grant through the DfES Standards Fund many local-authority treasurers took the opportunity to withdraw the LEA funds. With a guarantee of government funds only until 2008, and local authorities' budgets already fully committed, the issue of who is to subsidise instrumental tuition in schools remains unresolved. Wider opportunities to increase the number of pupils learning an instrument will be paid for by realigning the present provision – shorter lessons, larger teaching groups, and increased charges to parents. This policy will merely create a cohort of pupils disappointed by their parents' inability or unwillingness to pay for their lessons once the costs of tuition have to be met.

Partnership roles in music education thrive when they are built upon a foundation of understanding by both parties. Where this thrives the outcomes are greater than the sum total of individual effort.

## ■ Supporter

The supporter, whilst not directly in the activity of an enterprise, contributes and endorses its achievements. In music education it goes far beyond cheer leader, applause and an appreciative audience. Whilst the supporter offers a commitment comparable to that of the partnership role that we have explored, it has distinctive characteristics and features which we need to consider.

In the 1970s John Paynter developed and disseminated his Schools Council Project, based at York University where Wilfrid Mellers had revolutionised undergraduate music courses. John Paynter brought together some fifty young teachers who saw the need for change, shared their ideas, and exchanged news of successful classroom work. In a spirit of mutual support they transformed the secondary-school scene by encouraging their pupils to explore creative aspects of music-making and

8 DfES, *The Music Manifesto*, unpaginated.

perform the music of contemporary composers. The influence of these pioneers became evident and many soon found themselves in positions where they were able to shape the course of music education. It was a watershed which revealed, amongst other things, the significance of the contemporary composer in the classroom. Paynter recognised that the supporter role was an effective means to disseminate his ideas. Whilst he did promote his work through the written word, by far the greatest influence came through the teachers in project schools throughout the country, undertaking supporter roles for their colleagues.

An examination of three models will perhaps further illustrate the supporter role. Firstly, the splint – a support which is externally applied in order to allow the repair of a broken or damaged limb. It requires a diagnosis and then expert placement to effect a speedy recovery. It is temporary, allowing for its removal once the limb is fully healed, a process which may vary from patient to patient. The prime object of this support is restorative. Weak management of a music department or a lapse in a teacher's energy and initiative might qualify for temporary splint-support.

Scaffolding, however, fulfils a different purpose. It is erected externally in order to support initial building, or the redecoration or repair of an existing structure. It is adaptable to meet the size, shape and location of the principal structure. Once the building or redecoration has been completed, the scaffolding is removed and the process starts again somewhere else. This support is adaptable, flexible, easily transportable and, as with Paynter's project teachers, designed to suit specific circumstances. This model of support will be familiar to advisers, advisory teachers and a host of other pollinating agents, who have given support to individual teachers and to schools, with far greater influence than countless tons of documents from curriculum councils or agencies.

The scaffold-supporter model is to be found in enlightened structures for training future generations of musicians and teachers. Here the relationship between the principal and complementary roles seeks to take account of the changing environment – advances in technology, modified social patterns and values. This is not about replicating past edifices, rather it is creating a land with music in which the majority of musicians will have a 'portfolio career'. All music colleges now offer courses to sustain the portfolio – outreach and community, pedagogy, business and marketing skills. These are all buzz words in their curriculum. Some music educators regard this as cosmetic, others as revolutionary. The training of future leaders in conservatoires, which hitherto have focused almost exclusively upon the performer and composer, is beginning to take account of the broader range of functions. Perhaps one day some administrator will realise that they might also be the best place in which to train future teachers of music.

The scaffold-support model is in many respects adopted by funding agencies, such as the Lottery-funded Youth Music which provides resources and advice enabling bridges to be forged between in-school and out-of-school activities. There is a thriving scene of music-making, initiated by many different bodies, including pupils and students themselves, in informal settings outside the confines of the school curriculum. As the pressure grows for schools to develop a curriculum to include more subjects – citizenship, health and safety, and the like – decisions have to be taken about how to allocate the twenty-five hours a week for forty weeks a year. This makes a total of 15,000 hours of compulsory schooling. For a time-bound discipline like music this is a problem: there is no speed-reading in music, so if a piece takes eight minutes to perform, it cannot be condensed into two. Extra-curricular activities are not restricted like school classes to a single age-group, but draw upon the whole range of pupils, often from more than a single school: peer learning in practice.

Youth Music has developed its scaffolding to ensure that there is good preparation, through applying for grants, and through monitoring and evaluation before the support is moved on to the next initiative. However, restricting its definition of 'youth' to the under-eighteen-year-olds undoubtedly inhibits the development of post-school-age opportunities. It is a challenge to ensure that future scaffolding reaches beyond the first rung.

A buttress, my third model of support, is also external, but forms part of the structure sometimes incorporated into its design. It shores up, secures, and is often indistinguishable from, the principal structure itself. It is erected with the intention of being permanent. Those who work in music services, providing instrumental and vocal tuition for pupils and professional enrichment for teachers, apply their support in this mode. The success of a music service may be judged by the degree to which it integrates and becomes a part of the schools it serves whilst still retaining its own identity.

This selection of models of support has been made to underline significant features of the supporter and the supported, the principal and the complementary role partners. Understanding the objectives of each role is essential, and looking at models helps in this process. An advisory teacher who provides support in a school needs, from the outset, to ensure that the work will not crumble when they remove their splint-like support. At best the objective is to facilitate an independence for both the supported and supporter: success is measured after the point of departure. The duration needed for adequate support requires careful consideration. Over-dependence upon support structures can inhibit the ultimate repair, redecoration, or building.

Those who offer short-term support to schools in the form of projects for pupils or courses for teachers look for lasting outcomes. The supporter's comfortable feeling of a worthy engagement can quickly evaporate if nothing has been left behind – no reflection, no memories, no legacy. For this reason alone it is essential that the partners, supporter and supported, understand their roles, the prime aims of the engagement and the expected outcomes. This is not a complex matter. It does not require pages of educational jargon. Quite straightforwardly it is a matter of talking about roles: Who is going to do what, and when, and how? What are the expectations? And how will we know what has been achieved?

## ■ Conclusion

You might now be asking about the practical application of exploring various roles in music education. Models of splints and scaffolds, playing tennis or partnering dancers must be relevant to present-day functions in music education. I believe that the relevance is in the need for clarity and precision in defining responsibilities. This complex operation of music education today embraces far more than the straightforward instructed–instructor relationship of the early pioneers of nineteenth-century schooling, whose schools were rewarded by a system of payment by results: sixpence for six songs learned by rote, and sixpence for every child who could sing at sight.

Instrumental teachers, teaching assistants, higher-level teaching assistants, musicians, community musicians, students in training, animateurs and a host of others, qualified, unqualified and partly qualified, join the resident teacher in a school to nurture young musical interest and talent. Structures in higher education and the informal sector are no less complex.

It would be a mistake to seek a return to patterns which served past generations well. Today's challenge is, within the complex web of possibilities, for leaders, partners and supporters to ensure the nurturing of musical talent across all genres and cultural traditions, all social categorisations and all ages.

These roles are distinctive yet interdependent, exclusive, yet universal. They are multi-faceted. Rich in the potential of human interaction, they resonate with musical significance. Composers are the leaders who invite us to explore the territory of their creative imagination. Performers undertake a partnership with the composer as they embrace their role of interpreting and conveying musical significance. The listener plays the role of supporter, not as an ancillary or second fiddle, but as an integral part of the trilogy.

The future direction of music education will be influenced by our capacity to exercise our critical faculties and reflect upon current practices. By bringing our perspective of music education today into sharper focus we will continue to remind ourselves that each of the many players has a role to play.

### ■ A postscript for the new generation, 2011

Rereading what I wrote in 2004, I am struck by the number of changes which I would today have to recognise. The many music-education initiatives of our previous government – Sing Up, Wider Opportunities, In Harmony, Centres for Advanced Training, and many others, all seek to support and encourage. Doubtless many good things were achieved through these and other publically funded initiatives. However, what has become known as 'the banking crisis', and a change of government, have already left supportive, centralised initiatives in music education far behind. Perhaps the initiators failed to bring the schools on board with them, or they did not realise that funding from the centre, rather than from school budgets, is as vulnerable to political whim as is the cash from the public purse.

In the final paragraphs of my original text I recognised that each generation has to nurture musical talent and cultural traditions within 'a complex web of possibilities', not necessarily seeking to return to patterns that served in the past. The current wholesale axing of public funding for music education in schools and the imposition of a tax-levy on students, whether prompted by bankers' misjudgements or political ideology, presents music educators with a challenge so great, so overwhelming, that it appears to deny the very principles that shaped my own professional life and my own education.

*Fifth Bernarr Rainbow Lecture,*
*given at The Royal Over-Seas*
*League, London, 11 May 2010*

# Two-Score Years and Then?
# Reflections and Progressions from a
# Life in Participatory Music and Arts

GAVIN HENDERSON

Gavin Henderson grew up in Brighton, went to art schools at Brighton, Kingston and the Slade, and worked as a professional trumpeter. He has directed festivals at York, Bracknell, Brighton and Dartington (1985–2010). He was Principal of Trinity College of Music from 1994 to 2006, moving the College to the Old Royal Naval College in Greenwich and merging it with the Laban Centre for Dance. He has served on some of the most influential musical organisations, often as chair, has received honorary degrees or fellowships from several institutions, and he was made a CBE in 2004. He is now Principal of the Royal Central School of Speech and Drama.

I FEEL VERY HONOURED, and not a little daunted, to be giving this talk under the auspices of the Bernarr Rainbow Trust. As a former Principal of Trinity College of Music it was my privilege to bestow Honorary Fellowship upon Bernarr Rainbow in recognition of his untiring and inspirational work in music education. We were lucky to have Peter Dickinson as one of our Board Members at that time, and Peter has of course done so much to keep the influence of Bernarr Rainbow very much alive, not least in the support offered by the eponymous trust.

When we discussed the title for this talk, Peter was concerned that I might be straying from the spirit of educating the young, which lies at the heart of Bernarr Rainbow's philosophy. Whilst this is an element of what I wish to raise, I am also reflecting my own experience in what has been a diverse life in the arts – for some two-score years, and I hope it will continue for some time to come. So – Two-Score Years and Then? That question must also embrace the broad issue of how we engage with music as we pass from the intensity of a professional working life, normally of some two-score years, into what we now refer to as the Third Age.

A little over three-score years ago it was my good fortune to be born in Brighton, a town of raffish reputation, liberal attitude, and artistic inclination. Growing up in such a place, I thought that all towns would be much the same and only in my late teens did I realise this was not the case. I shared a paper round, for instance, which included the houses of Laurence Olivier and Joan Plowright, John Clements and Kay Hammond, Flora Robson, Dora Bryan, Sir Terence Rattigan, and the 'cheeky chappie' himself, Max Miller, little appreciating at the time the import of such clientele.

I suppose that my first musical encounter was an appearance on the stage of Brighton's fabulous old Hippodrome Theatre for a pantomime with Professor Jimmy Edwards, then star of a TV comedy series called *Whacko!* Set in a boys' school, if shown today it would probably have all the perpetrators facing prosecution. It was certainly not in tune with the kind of educational enlightenment that Bernarr Rainbow was striving for at much the same time, but an interesting barometer of how far popular perceptions have moved in the ensuing fifty years. Be that as it may, eight little children were invited onto the stage during *Goldilocks and the Three Bears*, and I was one of them. We each held a tiny plastic trumpet, each with a different note. As Jimmy Edwards tapped us variously on the head, we blew our trumpets, thus introducing the tune of the pantomime song which was then scrolled down for all to sing. It was perhaps not so far removed from some of the games played today in musical education and outreach projects. I longed for my own trumpet from that day on, a longing compounded by broadcasts of a popular entertainer of the time, who seemed to have only a couple of tunes in his repertoire. One was this:

> □   Eddie Calvert ('The Man with the Golden Trumpet') playing Paul
>     Burkhard, 'Oh My Papa' (1954)

It would be interesting to go round the room tonight and explore how differently music made an early impression, and just what was that first encounter that triggered a lifetime's interest. However much we seek to prescribe best practice, it will probably be a quite unexpected occasion which sets the pulse ticking in every sense.

In my own case it was in spite of my schooling. I have some sympathy with Osbert Sitwell's entry in *Who's Who* which stated: 'Education – between terms at Eton'. Aside from a little classroom singing – usually of *Bobby Shafto's Gone to Sea* – there was nothing up to the age of thirteen. I wanted to learn the trumpet, but was told I was too young. I suspect it had more to do with the paucity of teaching available to the school. In a colliery community or with the Salvation Army I would have had a cornet put in my hands from the age of five. How differently things are approached today, indeed how differently I think I would have been treated at that time if I had been in a state school in Brighton. There a vibrant instrumental teaching service was emerging, feeding into one of the earliest established youth orchestras, driven by the visionary Head of Education in Brighton, W. G. Stone. By a happy coincidence he eventually became Principal of Central School of Speech and Drama, the post I hold today. But five decades ago was the period of post-war optimism that was to lead to the halcyon years of music education, manifest in the Inner London Education Authority for instance, and in many other local authorities as well.

As my schooling developed things improved with the arrival of an inspirational head of music – Jack Hindmarsh – but not before an array of school reports described me as 'no academic'. The science master wrote: 'Wonderfully bad – chemistry to Gavin is like the firm next door with which we have no connection'. The housemaster rounded off with a disappointed few lines to the effect that I would never be a flyer and was no team player. Perhaps this related to my desultory interest in sport and by way of afterthought he added: 'maybe Gavin could do something with his art and music'. We had no school orchestra, so I could never have experienced what is probably the most sophisticated and inspiring process of teamwork – that of playing in an orchestra. How differently things are viewed today – but just as Brighton College prides itself on first-rate musical tuition and achievement in the arts generally, the local authority music service is bracing itself for the prospect of serious cuts in government funding.

Under Jack Hindmarsh various initiatives were nurtured, notably with the choir. As a treble I sang a Pickled Boy in Britten's *St Nicolas*, and a series of concerts by visiting chamber groups brought contact with professional musicians. I remember going to one such concert at a time when I was feeling very dejected about school life and suddenly I was caught by a particular piece, which absolutely lifted my spirits. It was as though it was speaking to me personally, and seemed so perfectly formed that anything else I was suffering at the time seemed insignificant. It is a work I have come back to again and again at times of conflict or depression and it never fails to revive me:

☐ W. A. Mozart, Flute Quartet in D major, K285

I did get to study the trumpet, with a member of the Hippodrome Band, and joined the Brighton Youth Orchestra. There I met friends from further afield and a number of students from Sussex University, just being launched, and I remained a member once I moved on to Brighton Art College. There were also a number of little amateur orchestras of older players, many retired from the light music and ballroom scene, and even some from the silent cinema days, passing on a unique experience which has now all but vanished. For a summer job I washed glasses in the Ocean Bar at the end of the Palace Pier, where Percy Warden and his orchestra entertained the drinkers. I had asked for a request of 'These Foolish Things Remind Me of You' and this became something of a regular feature. Each evening Percy Warden would announce: 'For the young man washing the glasses – we'll now play "These Foolish Things Remind Me of You".' And so it went on. I got the job again the following summer but, sadly, cuts had reduced the entertainment to Percy Warden at the piano, no orchestra, but he remembered me and the whole thing started again with 'These Foolish Things'. Then, one rain-swept night, he was not there; a 'dep' was playing the piano for the few bedraggled and drenched customers. At the break I told him of our little tradition – would he mind playing 'These Foolish Things'? 'With great pleasure', he said, and played it beautifully. He then came back to the bar and asked if I would like a drink. Shaking my hand, he said: 'My name's Jack Strachey: I wrote that song.' A very Brighton incident.

☐ Jack Strachey and Eric Maschwitz, 'These Foolish Things' (1936)

I suppose Jack Strachey was the first composer I ever met, but that would soon change. I became fascinated in the story of an octogenarian composer living along the coast at Shoreham, who had composed a large number of symphonies for impossibly large forces. So I went and introduced myself to the very reclusive Havergal Brian. We talked about many things to do with his early years in the potteries, and how he came to Brighton and there composed his gargantuan *Gothic Symphony*, but he was fascinated by my connection with the piers. Brian said that his very first symphony had been premiered by the West Pier Orchestra in the early 1920s, under the flamboyant Lyell Taylor, who addressed his audience on the Monday morning to announce the new work by Mr Havergal Brian: 'It is probably above your heads so I propose to play it every day this week and twice on Saturday.' Quite an object lesson for all who strive so hard for the promotion of new music with, perhaps, little chance of a second or third performance.

I know that I am in danger of drifting into another talk that I have given many times about seaside piers and entertainment, but there are a few aspects to share with you as to what we have lost, and what we may yet gain, from the example of these traditions. Some of the retired players I met through the various amateur orchestras spoke of their days at the seaside and spa – there would be no rehearsal, you had to sight-read everything and often be prepared to transpose. A seaside orchestra might have a familiarising session at the beginning of the season, and maybe some vestigial rehearsal with a visiting soloist, but otherwise it was eyes down for two or three sessions a day, with much music being freshly composed or arranged. In many cases the musical director would bring his own library with him. It was an extraordinary training ground and I believe that this is where the great British reputation for expert sight-reading springs from. It is a skill which in due course furnished the commercial-recording and film-soundtrack world, where such speed and efficiency was cost-effective compared to the working practices in other countries. No one was specifically trained to sight-read at such a pace. They simply learnt on the job – and perhaps we are now losing the edge as there is no raw culture feeding the system.

The Bournemouth Symphony Orchestra was born out of this tradition, but one of the last of the typical resort-based orchestras was the Worthing Municipal Orchestra, and as I gradually started to play professionally this was my first regular work. The core of the orchestra was just eight musicians, playing essentially palm court selections during the week, and then they would add players for weekend concerts and special occasions. I well remember playing the *1812 Overture* with an orchestra specially augmented to fifteen players. We also played for seasons of grand opera in the Pier Pavilion, as well as light opera and Gilbert and Sullivan. Worthing also had a fine repertory theatre company – The Connaught – with which we collaborated. As the traditional holiday fare declined, so the orchestra, and indeed the theatre, adapted. We did a combined tour of Stravinsky's *The Soldier's Tale*, for instance, around local schools. The musical director was responsible for a large-scale amateur orchestra within which the Municipal Orchestra members would play and coach. He would also train the regular choir and choral society. It was becoming something of a model, but alas the changing times would eventually see both the Municipal Orchestra and the theatre company disbanded. It was an elderly community; there was no youth orchestra as such; but the Citizens' Orchestra, the large amateur group led by the professional players of the Municipal Orchestra, combined all ages. Had such arts provision continued, we might have witnessed something on the lines of what Pierre Boulez has called for in an 'ensemble of possibilities'.[1] It is an ironic coincidence that Pierre Boulez's first ever appearance with the BBC Symphony Orchestra was at Worthing; another coincidence is that Harold Pinter was living in the town.

Brighton could be said to have lagged behind, but this would change with the founding of the Brighton Festival in 1967 which, from its earliest days, was a vibrant force. Here too the piers played their part. Malcolm Williamson, for instance, led youth workshops in musical theatre with *The Moonrakers* and his children's opera *Julius Caesar Jones* in the Palace Pier Theatre. One thinks of educational projects from the opera houses as being a relatively recent phenomenon – and someone like Malcolm Williamson is certainly out of fashion today – but what was going on then was really quite ground-breaking. Working as an assistant on the Brighton Festival was amongst my earliest work in arts production, and one of the projects I was involved with was the 1969 premiere of Harrison Birtwistle's first music theatre piece, *Down by the Greenwood Side*, to a libretto by Michael Nyman, in a double bill with *Façade*. This was on the West Pier. It was quite

---

1 Pierre Boulez, *Boulez on Music Today*, trans. Susan Bradshaw and Richard Rodney Bennett (London: Faber, 1971), pp. 35–6.

an ordeal, with stage and technical rehearsals going on late into the night. Birtwistle remembers two old gentlemen coming in at the back of the hall chatting away at a rather tense moment in the rehearsal. He turned and chided them: 'Look, you've got the whole Pier to talk on: why can't you just shove off and leave us to our work?' Then something made him look round again, and he realised it was Laurence Olivier and William Walton.

That same year Richard Attenborough shot the first film he directed, *Oh, What a Lovely War!*, on the two Brighton Piers – it was something of an epitaph, for the West Pier closed soon after.

    □  Bert Lee and R. P. Weston, 'Goodbye-ee', from *Oh, What a Lovely War!* (1963)

I worked as an extra on the film, and also played in the pit for a revival of the show with Joan Littlewood at the Theatre Royal, Stratford East. Whilst I could have gone to a music college, I chose instead to go to art school. I have always felt that we segregate our arts and little is done to explore relationships between the various disciplines. It was also true, less so now, that the music conservatoires were very conservative. At an art school you would be working afresh, creating of the moment: at music college you would be intensively practising well-established repertoire. I was also able to maintain a semi-professional existence as a trumpet player and did so increasingly in baroque music, though before the period instrument specialism took root. That was to come later.

At the Slade we embarked on early forms of performance art, which bemused the likes of William Coldstream, the head of the School; Reg Butler, my tutor for sculpture; and Anthony Gross, who taught etching. There was a remarkable artist who did appreciate one's interest in other art forms – the painter Robert Medley, who had been a founding figure in the Group Theatre for which Britten and Auden had first collaborated. With Medley's assistance I gained a travelling scholarship to America, basically hung out in New York across a whole summer, and there met a remarkable group of artists, musicians and dance and theatre practitioners. There was a much easier sense of synergy and partnership across all the arts, perhaps best manifested in the collaboration of John Cage with Merce Cunningham and Robert Rauschenberg, and in the multi-art work of Robert Wilson, for which everything starts with the discipline of drawing. In New York I met and established an enduring friendship with the composer and critic Virgil Thomson, whose surreal operas that began with Gertrude Stein's *Four Saints in Three Acts* seemed to epitomise a collaborative ideology.

    ☐  Virgil Thomson, 'Pigeons on the Grass Alas', from *Four Saints in Three Acts* (1934)

I came back from New York determined to work for the sense of a multi-skilled ensemble in performance; for wider participation in the making of new work; and for some means by which the arts could specifically influence the structure and life of a community. And so it was that I got a job at the Victoria Theatre, Stoke-on-Trent, as assistant front-of-house and publicity manager. I needed to get experience in administration, but was drawn to this theatre which had been established by the pioneer of theatre-in-the-round Stephen Joseph, and was now renowned for its creation of documentary theatre based on local issues, led by Peter Cheeseman. It was here that a young string quartet was embarking on a residency at Keele University, taking its name from the University's first vice-chancellor – The Lindsay. I had also been drawn to Stoke through a love of Arnold Bennett, whose Five Towns novels were dramatised at the Vic., and there was also the connection with Havergal Brian who became the subject of one of the theatre's documentaries. Whilst it provided a wonderful grounding in basic management, there was not the scope to be involved directly in the productions, and so I moved on to festivals. I created a first foray into the arts for the new town of Crawley and then moved to York where, thanks to the brave advocacy of Wilfrid Mellers, I became Director of the York Festival and Mystery Plays at the tender age of twenty-three.

Whilst the appointment at York may have been accidental and opportunistic, it was also providential. Firstly there were the Mystery Plays – the very foundation of English theatre based on the participation of literally hundreds of local people. In medieval times each of the forty-two plays was cast from a trade guild and trundled around the streets on wagon stages to a succession of stations, where the audience remained to await each play. In the post-war revivals they were performed with a massive cast in the panoramic setting of the ruins of St Mary's Abbey. But I wanted to get back to the spirit of the itinerant ensembles and so commissioned a mobile street opera from John Paynter, one of the many composers whom

Wilfrid Mellers had gathered around him at the University of York. It was a piece created for and by local children. If I had lacked any formal higher-education training in music, I made up for it by the ready welcome extended to all manner of activities at the university music department, with friendships established that have informed the rest of my working life. But above all, the York experience was one of really understanding the impact that can be made by a community coming together for the creation of a major celebration through the arts. One of the projects I was drawn into was the university's performance of the Monteverdi *Vespers* of 1610. They had one trumpeter as a student, and his name was John Wallace. They needed a second. It is a work that has ever since permeated my various professional roles.

☐ Claudio Monteverdi, *Vespers* (1610)

Within my time at York I also became Chief Executive of what was then the New Philharmonia Orchestra, and happily, in due course, appointed John Wallace as its principal trumpet. To describe the process of renewal that we went through at that time, including re-establishment of the orchestra's original name, is another story. Today we take the educational work of orchestras for granted. It is a real achievement of the last twenty-five years, but in 1975 it was unheard of. With the support of the Musicians' Union we launched a series of educational outreach projects with regional youth orchestras, and then we also embarked upon a number of significant residencies, notably in Nottinghamshire, with educational outreach being as vital as the concerts we gave. The London Sinfonietta is often credited with being the originator of orchestral education work; indeed, it did establish the first dedicated officer to lead such work. But it was not the first in the field. Simon Rattle was engaged for his first work with a London orchestra, and he conducted our commission of Peter Maxwell Davies's first symphony at one of the Nottinghamshire residences, with Max leading workshops and pre-concert activity.

☐ Peter Maxwell Davies, Symphony no. 1 (1976)

One of the issues which I found frustrating was the sense of detachment which an orchestra such as the Philharmonia had from its public at that time, and still does to a large extent, within the context of the Royal Festival

Hall. I missed the kind of integration with a distinct community that characterised the theatre in Stoke and the festival at York. So I went to Bracknell to develop the South Hill Park Arts Centre, and built the Wilde Theatre as part of it. As a new town, Bracknell was something of a blank canvas, just as Crawley had been, in terms of arts provision. Clearly there was a temptation to build a major auditorium, by way of civic pride, but this was resisted in favour of a place where people could come to participate. Our slogan was 'Do It at The Park' – and they did. On a TV documentary about The Park I claimed that market research showed that 90 per cent of the people of Bracknell used their arts centre in one form or another. One of our greatest supporters, a local doctor, came in and berated me for this:

'Successful it is, of course, but you'll win no friends with such blatant exaggeration.'

'Well, that's what the research came up with', I said.

'Tell you what, I'll ask all my patients tomorrow if they come to The Park.'

The following night he called in. 'You win: the figure's actually 100 per cent.'

What was not obvious was the level of daytime participation ranging from a pre-school, arts-centred playgroup through to a series of late starter's programmes. South Hill Park embraced a cradle-to-grave ethos, with many generations intermingling.

For some reason our national psyche rejects such positive statistics. We seem peculiarly averse to celebrating our cultural achievements – as was manifest in the run up to the general election of 2010. A recent poll commissioned by the Incorporated Society of Musicians through YouGov showed that 91 per cent of adults believe that every child should have the opportunity to learn a musical instrument in school – not something which we heard politicians doing much to pledge. Why do they so distrust such public opinion? We are all aware of the compelling evidence showing the benefit of musical education in terms of general cognitive behaviour; of the confidence that is honed through participation in music; and of the hugely cost-effective results which involvement in music can bring to a society increasingly worried about knife crime, gang warfare, and vandalism. We admire and applaud the considerable achievement of the Venezuelan model El Sistema in countering the terrible effects of poverty and deprivation, but do not seem able to translate this into anything other than a relatively marginal commitment to our own musical endeavour. We fail to acknowledge the cause and effect of a period in which escalation of youth crime and drug abuse parallels the erosion of arts-based activity, and music education in particular, that was once an example to the rest of the world. Indeed we are bracing ourselves for possibly significant cuts to the support of local-authority music services which have fought bravely to rebuild from the county music structure that was lost during the Thatcher years. I was at Bracknell at that time, and the arts centre was able to do much to bring about interconnection with schools and to promote the cause of young people's music-making. Though we mourned the withdrawal of the well-resourced music education system that had been the envy of the world, the pressure to survive did bring about a range of new partnerships.

After Bracknell I worked in tandem as Director of the Brighton Festival and the Dartington International Summer School – in both cases drawn by the possibilities of bringing together the best in professional practice and leadership with the participation of many others. I left Brighton to go to Trinity College of Music, with something of a mission to nurture the kind of versatile musician who could work both as performer and animateur, and to seek recognition from the Higher Education Funding Council that such a professional musician merited training at the highest level. Ronald Reagan once said, 'You can achieve anything in this world provided that you don't mind who gets the credit for it'. And so it was in this instance. I needed others to make the case for us, and engineered an enquiry commissioned jointly by the Higher Education Funding Council for England and Youth Music, which resulted in the report *Creating a Land with Music*.[2] The report achieved exactly what it was hoped it would, and whilst many of the conservatoires questioned its direction at the time, few would now disagree with the essence of its recommendations, and most would claim to be leaders in the field of fostering the holistic and creative musician.

An earlier report commissioned by the Gulbenkian Foundation,

2 Rick Rogers, *Creating a Land with Music: The Work, Education and Training of Musicians in the 21st Century* (London: Higher Education Funding Council for England, 2002).

published in 1997, called *Joining In* had underpinned the potential for a more participatory culture. At that time I was a member of the Arts Council and Chairman of its Music Panel. Reading the report, I became concerned about the lack of any reference to the education authorities and the ministry: it was all about what the Arts Council and the then Regional Arts Boards should be doing. I realised that one had reasonable access to the arts authorities but no real access to the high command in education. The new Secretary of State was David Blunkett – since he was blind one had to find a way of getting things proposed to him. I took the report home to Brighton to read more carefully over the weekend, but got more and more concerned about the need to get the issue of music education, and instrumental tuition in particular, raised with Blunkett. But how to get to him? Early on the Sunday morning, I was digging in my little garden thinking about how to cut through the bureaucracy, when the French windows onto the balcony of the house next door opened, and out came a black Labrador dog, followed by David Blunkett. 'Good God!', I said, 'Mr Blunkett!' And he was, needless to say, somewhat shocked and surprised. I told him of my concerns. 'You'll probably think this is a set up', I said. And he replied, 'Yes, it is a bit improbable.' But eventually he was convinced. He was in Brighton for the Labour Party Conference and needed a safe house for him and his dog Lucy. He spoke of his own concern for instrumental teaching and I told him of the Lottery pot which I had just been put in charge of by the Arts Council and then Secretary of State, Chris Smith, to create a Youth Music Trust. It was assumed that this £10m per year would fix the cause of music tuition, but I stressed that this could not be the case. We had to find a way of rebuilding something of the nearly £200m that had been lost by way of the disbanded County Council Music System.

He asked me specifically to write to him care of his constituency office and not via the DES, as it was then. I did so and he was as good as his word. We met and, whilst I cannot claim that that exchange over the garden wall gave rise to the Standards Fund, this did in due course emerge and left us free to create a somewhat maverick new organisation that is now flourishing as Youth Music, under the directorship of Christina Coker.

It was a contentious development. The music services that had emerged in difficult circumstances to fill the vacuum left by the abolition of the old County Council structure, and had fought valiantly to bring the opportunity of instrumental tuition to all sections of society, felt that they should have this Lottery money. But I hope they have come to realise the value of an organisation that has brokered many new relationships, particularly in what is best described as informal education. It has been criticised for being party to a general dumbing-down process, but its main brief has been to open up first access to participation in music, and not to focus on the high end of achievement. That said, it has fought for proper resourcing of the national youth organisations – the National Youth Orchestra and Music for Youth – and also for establishing a national youth programme for South Asian music. In ten years Youth Music has reached around two and a half million young people, and more recently it has taken responsibility for the government-funded initiative Sing Up, which has nurtured singing through the primary schools of England with a take-up of some 86 per cent. But this, as with so many special programmes, is time limited and will cease, in this initial round, in 2011. It was the product of the so-called 'Music Manifesto', a means of lobbying government. I hope that our new government will keep that manifesto very much in its sights.

A decade on, ominous noises are being made about moving the responsibility for instrumental teaching out of the education budget and into the arts sector. It has been suggested that Youth Music might take this on. I do not suppose I will get another chance to nobble a Secretary of State over the garden wall, but it behoves us all to lobby the cause, for not only is instrumental teaching under threat once again, but so too is the place of music in the National Curriculum. It would be very dangerous to lose music, and indeed the cross-section of arts practice, from out of the ring-fenced education sector.

I am not by any means against a better relationship between the publicly funded arts sector and that of education. The experience at Dartington has made me convinced of the need to bring people of all generations together to participate in the making of music. The twentieth century did wonders in bringing the best of all performances to everyone by means of recording and broadcasting – but it also anaesthetised and inhibited much that was previously delivered within the community. Music became a commodity – something to take rather than something to make – and this has been compounded for those reaching retirement, who are not so easily exposed to a system of music education. We now live in a society where different agendas are addressed for the respective extremes of age. Where once it was common for people of all ages to sing in a choir or play in a band, now we are facing increasing segregation. Dartington Summer School has highlighted the real joy that can come from people of all ages and abilities working together, nowhere more so than in the non-auditioned choir. Each week they assemble for an hour and a half after breakfast, and on Friday they are joined by the orchestra; that evening they give the closing concert of the week. The conductor has no idea what the relative standard will be, or the balance of the voices. But it has been a wonderful training ground. The conductors who have braved this random approach include Colin Davis, Andrew Davis, Simon Rattle, Richard Hickox, Mark Elder, John Eliot Gardiner, Roger Norrington, and George Malcolm – not to mention Benjamin Britten, Aaron Copland, and Malcolm Arnold. We have tried to explore unusual repertoire, forgotten works that were once part of the great choral tradition: for instance, Gounod's *Messe Solennelle*, a work I have played in for over forty-five consecutive Easter Sundays at St Bartholomew's Church, Brighton. I never tire of this lovely *benedictus*:

☐ Charles-François Gounod, 'Benedictus', from *Messe Solennelle* (1854)

If we think we have an emerging crisis in terms of music education for the young, it is nothing compared to what will have to be addressed as the age profile of our population shifts in the coming years. Today there are four working people for every retired person; in forty-five years there will be just two. In terms of taxable resource to provide for such a change, it is unsustainable. We have to create a society and a culture which is not driven by such division, and we need to start cultivating that now. Forty-five years may seem a long way off, but this issue is gathering momentum, and just think how far we have advanced in the last forty-five years since the days of Jimmy Edwards in *Whacko!* Indeed, two-score years from then.

I make no apology for introducing the issue of popular culture and the difficulty faced for so-called 'high art' and classical music. Much can be made of the impact of the creative industries to the UK economy, although this tends not to feature in the representations of the CBI, largely because each element is so comparatively small. We do not conform easily with sectors like the pharmaceutical and motor industries, or financial services, but we do make up the second largest part of the commercial wellbeing of the country. This was before the collapse of the largest sector – banking and financial services. Unlike other areas of commerce, ours is a sector that is still growing, at something like 4 per cent per annum. It is fed by a vigorous education system. Disturb it at your economic peril! Music alone represents some £5 billion a year, of which export earnings are around £1.3 billion. But we have to recognise that this is not essentially driven by classical music. The establishment of TV, hi-fi, and now super-efficient mobile systems is something common to all, largely a post-war phenomenon. In this time we have also witnessed the implementation of publicly funded arts support. It interests me that the Arts Council was born out of the wartime CEMA (Council for the Encouragement of Music and the Arts), whilst no succession was established for the light-entertainment system called ENSA (Entertainments National Service Association – or commonly referred to as Every Night Something Awful). Understandably perhaps, as this was specifically directed at the Forces.

What we can see is the growth in recorded and broadcast music, increasingly driven by commercial advantage, with music becoming something to collect. Where once we looked forward to a new work, just as we look forward to a new novel and play, now we compare different versions of established masterworks. Public funding increasingly came to the rescue of new initiatives, to support commissioning of the more challenging repertoire which had alienated, or been alienated by, the marketplace of popular culture. What was once the underground of rebellious artists became a new establishment of contemporary performance, especially in music, with funding directed by a new form of bureaucracy – arts administration. The work was protected by subsidy and the artists' need to communicate was effectively negated. I well remember my friend the late Michael Vyner proudly claiming that only his orchestra, the London Sinfonietta, was really able to play such and such a composer's work. What, I wondered, had our society come to when we could not perceive of a new work as something we might join with others in making together – as a shared experience of participation?

Much has changed with the onset of educational outreach programmes driven by the various orchestras, arts centres, festivals and opera companies. Perhaps initially as a means of marketing, for the wooing of new audiences, this work has come centre stage as part of the core function of the organisation, rather than a peripheral piece of public relations and audience development. Composers have relished the chance to work with diverse communities of participants, and perhaps a new era of engagement has dawned, now also fed by the revolution in interactive technology. The National Curriculum has helped in giving attention to creative music-making. In little more than a decade Youth Music has cultivated a role for the animateur, with some 16,000 people supported to work as leaders in so called music-maker programmes. The country is now networked into a structure of Music Action Zones – partnerships of music-producing organisations across all genres. But Youth Music has a cut-off age of eighteen. Streams of specialised bureaucracy have developed around particular strata of education and youth provision, with understandable but now extreme layers of protection which inevitably frustrate the way in which young and old can intermingle. Inspirational artists can only gain full benefit from teaching if they have undertaken dedicated teacher training and gained the appropriate certification.

It is sad that our systems of accreditation and accountability can so restrict the involvement of many fine performers as teachers. This does not affect learning outside the formal sector so much and one must applaud the work of an organisation such as COMA (Contemporary Music for Amateurs) – a victim of short-sighted Arts Council cuts – and programmes for those in later life such as the Cobweb Orchestra in Durham, the Silver Song Club, or the RTO – that is, the Really Terrible Orchestra in Edinburgh, whose contrabassoon player is the author of *The No. 1 Ladies' Detective Agency*, Alexander McCall Smith. These are wonderful hybrids, but they are in the main exclusive to those in, or approaching, the Third Age.

It was heartening to read of the call from a range of arts organisations, led by the Voluntary Arts Network, the National Campaign for the Arts, and The National Association of Local Government Arts Officers, for greater grass roots participation in the arts. But where was this in the various political manifestos we have been subjected to? It cannot be long before election campaigns have to address the needs of the ageing population, not simply the very elderly and infirm, but the vigorous third-agers who have much to give to the young. In this we have much to learn from cultures in Africa and in Asia.

The experience of 'informal education' at Bracknell, and particularly in the Summer School at Dartington, in tandem with a working life in formal education, has shown me the great joy, natural synergy and benefit that comes from cross generational participation and informal learning, often led by performing artists who are not first and foremost teachers or academics. I wonder how long it will be before the chloroform of legislative regulation frustrates this sector? There are some wonderful recent initiatives to cherish – The Sage at Gateshead, for instance, where learning and participation are stitched into the fabric of a new centre for all kinds of music, for all ages and abilities, and where a new kind of contract for the players in the Northern Sinfonia is based on both performing and teaching – so close to what the late-lamented Worthing Orchestra so nearly became.

I began this talk in a negative frame about my initial schooling, and, whilst we listened to 'Oh My Papa', I neglected to credit the great warmth and encouragement I got from my father. As a school teacher, he was a linguist and a great sportsman; I am neither. He did, however, love listening to music. He played me all his old 78s and took me to concerts. He was no performer, but as a true Scot through and through, there was one song of the great Harry Lauder that he would render towards the end of a party. Today it could be a rallying call, as once again we marshal our efforts in the struggle for continued support and funding for the cause of music education and the arts in general.

☐   Harry Lauder, 'Keep Right on to the End of the Road' (1924)

PART II

# THE 2005 ROYAL PHILHARMONIC SOCIETY LECTURE

*Royal Philharmonic Society Lecture,*
*given at the Queen Elizabeth Hall,*
*London, 24 April 2005*

# Will Serious Music Become Extinct?

## SIR PETER MAXWELL DAVIES

Sir Peter Maxwell Davies was born in Salford, Greater Manchester, and was appointed Master of the Queen's Music in 2004, which widened the scope of the international reputation he had already enjoyed for at least three decades. He studied in Manchester and Rome and was then music master at Cirencester Grammar School (1959–62). With Harrison Birtwistle he founded the Pierrot Players, later the Fires of London, in 1967. He moved to the Orkney Islands in 1971; ten years later he was made CBE, and he was knighted in 1987.

THE OTHER EVENING, after my usual full day of writing music, I turned on BBC Radio 3, and was immediately immersed in Bach's *St Matthew Passion*. I felt privileged to be put so easily into touch with one of the greatest creative minds in our history, which had drawn together into one glowing, unified whole such diverse cultural threads – religious, historical and literary, alongside musical traditions. I reflected that through education I have access to all this, while at the same time regretting that the vast majority of people are unaware of it: not only unaware, but sometimes antagonistic, deeming it élitist, irrelevant to contemporary life, the product of a long-dead European white male.

I know the Bible upon which the work is based; I understand the German text; I know something of the rather peculiar Protestant theology permeating Bach's work; and the polyphonic and baroque traditions are familiar enough to enable me to appreciate efforts to create the original sound-world of the music. Most importantly – I can read music.

I reflected further that much of Bach's output, in common with so much of his age and before, was written for the resources of a relatively small town, to be performed immediately, as ritual, by and for ordinary people, where all members of society had, in theory, access to major musical experiences. Each town had at least one competent Kappelmeister, and although Bach, particularly, had one eye on God and eternity, he and his contemporaries were thoroughly practical in making music within the comprehension of its original executants and listeners, while often stretching them without compromise. It is clear for whom Bach was writing – God on the one hand, and his colleagues, performers and congregation on the other. If a Kappelmeister held a court position, too, so much the healthier for his working environment.

I can even record that broadcast performance of the *St Matthew Passion*, or buy a commercial recording. This is the first time the music of the past – and that of the present – has been available to all. The majority out there may be unaware of Bach, but we must not forget that he reaches, with international performances, broadcasts and recordings, an audience huge beyond his imagining, part of a phenomenon unprecedented in music's history.

But for whom do so-called serious, or classical, composers write now?

Before I embark upon conditions today, I would like to express my own view of the historical reasons for the increasing distance between composer, performer and audience in much of the previous century. This was to do with the breakdown of tonality, the fracture of rhythmic structure, and the paradoxically extremely Romantic attitude of composers who, while rejecting the principles of classical and Romantic musical composition, were prepared to write for a very small audience of like-minded listeners in tune with their sound-world.

The early twentieth-century collapse of the tonal system of related key-centres in art music, whose fall-out affects all of us, was regarded positively by many, often even as historically inevitable. Established hierarchies were undermined by ever more frequent changes of key. The fragmentation of rhythm meant that the ear could not cope with sequences of note-lengths unrelated to heartbeat or to any regular metre. Moreover, after World War II, musical form, so dependent upon memory to make connections and comparisons, changed far beyond anything envisaged by Schoenberg in *Erwartung*, or in his other early works where repetition of material was avoided.

In his *Technique de mon langage musical*, Messiaen expounds his influential rhythmic theories where 'rhythm' is dealt with as a unilinear sequence of note-values each of which can be augmented or diminished at will, building rhythmic 'personages' quite unlike anything in classical music.[1] If we think of any rhythm in the simplest unaccompanied melody, such as a Bach violin partita, we realise it cannot be written down merely as a line of note-values: the pitches are indivisible from their rhythmic function, with an implied pulse, an implied harmonic rhythm, and an internal hierarchy of four-bar phrases and eight-bar sentences. The point I am making is that the rhythm of pre-twentieth-century European art music cannot be expressed in a single line of note-values, but that it is intimately bound up with the pitches through which it is expressed with the tonic, or main key-note, acting as the rough equivalent of a vanishing point in visual perspective.

In musical form-building in the eighteenth and nineteenth centuries, such tools were taken for granted, and enabled composers to build formal structures in sonatas, quartets, concertos and symphonies – tools the equivalent of those used in the architecture of cathedrals and palaces from medieval times on. When the usefulness of such tools is questioned, and their application undermined or ignored through ignorance, the consequences can be literally shattering, as the baby disappears down the drain with the bath-water.

In the 50s and 60s of the last century it was common to see the century-defining musical revolution as having been initiated *c.* 1913 by Stravinsky's *Le Sacre* and Schoenberg's *Pierrot Lunaire*, with glances back to Debussy, Wagner and Liszt. For some people this revolution became related to concepts in communist practice under Stalin and Mao. In my time as a student in Italy in the late fifties, all Italian composers of my generation were communist. They thought the public would eventually be persuaded. Among the most *avant* of the *avant-garde*, nothing before Anton Webern was worth considering. Particularly demonised was the audience at Schoenberg's *Verklärte Nacht* of 1899 in Vienna, which hissed at an unprepared dissonance, thus demonstrating their bourgeois backwardness and decadence. Fifty years later, in a lecture given at the University of California and subsequently published in *Style and Idea* Schoenberg claimed that 'the emancipation of the dissonance – I mean the

---

1 Olivier Messiaen, *Technique de mon langage musical* (Paris: A. Leduc, 1944; in English, 1956).

comprehensibility of the discord – is equal to the comprehensibility of the concord.'

In the 1950s and 1960s the new music audiences I encountered would have had great difficulty in recognising an unprepared dissonance among the fragmented plethora of notes swirling past. In Vienna, one must remember that well into the twentieth century there was a tradition of *Hausmusik* – the bourgeoisie met to play chamber music together as good amateurs, so that a literate knowledge of music was then very common.

In Britain by the 1960s and 1970s there was a healthy amateur choral tradition throughout the country, and decent music education in schools. This ensured that many young people could read a line of music competently. There was plenty happening, with choral and instrumental groups, brass bands, a flourishing church music scene (particularly in the cathedrals), a culture of youth orchestras, and an increasingly wide interest in folk music. However, the younger generation of serious classical composers by and large hardly engaged with all of that, and there was precious little cross-fertilisation between the so-called *avant-garde* and what for most people counted as real music. This was to everybody's, and to music's, loss. Those who frequented contemporary classical concerts did so with commendable enthusiasm, and sometimes in most encouraging numbers. I remember splendid encounters with Stockhausen, Cage, Boulez and others when the BBC Promenade Concerts were under William Glock's direction, where one could believe, perhaps, that they demonstrated the way new music would turn in the future.

However, the nature of the listening experience was hardly up to the standard of the Viennese audience for *Verklärte Nacht*. Prepared or unprepared dissonances were accepted *en bloc* uncritically, listeners engaging with densities of texture (not harmony), speed of articulation, height or depth of tessitura, but scarcely encountering either long-term architectural design, or short-term phrase and sentence pattern. All this is inevitable when certain parameters involving memory are absent, making it impossible for the usual musical processes to create expectations. The language was vivid, exciting, and stimulating in new ways, but ultimately blunter, and in particular less suitable for the construction of large-scale architecture – the equivalent of cathedrals in sound. It was as if the vanishing of the tonal centre, and of the rhythmic hierarchies of tonal music, had brought all events to the music's surface, any interior dimensions having to be read or projected into the sound by the listener, much as, with the disappearance of perspective in abstract art, one finds oneself reading multidimensionality and perspective into a flat surface.

Since then, many composers have tried to rectify this situation, writing large works as well as music for school or amateur use, reintroducing elements into their work which are part of an ongoing musical *lingua franca*. One must also not forget that there were and are many composers who never subscribed to the revolution in the first place. In my adopted home, Scotland, Judith Weir, Sally Beamish, James MacMillan and some younger composers have been getting through to a sizeable minority.

The audiences at the BBC Promenade Concerts continue to welcome new works, so that one wonders where these people have gone when a Festival Hall or Barbican concert with new music is half empty or worse. This is in sorry contrast to other artforms: when a new play, novel or exhibition is announced, enough of the general public respond to make the enterprise successful. It is also depressing how many guests on *Desert Island Discs*, whose work in their own field one admires, choose no classical music whatsoever, while displaying familiarity and even erudition in other cultural fields

The root causes for this have to do with the historical background I outlined, but how does one explain the antipathy or downright opposition felt towards new serious music? Many concert-giving bodies, from symphony orchestras to local music societies, have a knee-jerk reaction to a proposed performance of, say, a work of mine: 'We can't possibly do that, the audience will stay away, and those that don't will hate it.' And I am a relatively well-known and established composer.

Successive governments have cut back on music education in state schools to the extent that music specialists have become a rarity. It is not uncommon for large schools at primary and secondary level to have no music specialist. This is very much a question of teacher training: some teachers cannot read or write musical notation and may be unaware of the world of classical music. Can we imagine the teaching of English in circumstances where the teacher not only does not know any poems, novels or plays, but cannot even read?

I do not advocate force-feeding children with a culture of classical music. One has only to think of all the people put off Shakespeare or Mozart after bad teaching at school. I have often said that a place cannot come to life musically until the inhabitants perform their own music. Moreover, there can be no real understanding of music without creating it. Can one imagine teaching art without ever encouraging children to draw, paint and make sculptures?

In my time as a school-teacher in 1959–62, at Cirencester, in a state grammar school, it became clear to me that, given the opportunity, nearly all children can improvise and compose music, in groups and individually. In a school of 500 or so boys and girls, I had a school orchestra, a junior orchestra, a choir of about forty, which could perform standard repertory, or be expanded to over 200 for a work like the Monteverdi *Vespers*. The sixth-formers founded a small choir called 'Pro Musica Optima' (as if my choir wasn't!) to sing more difficult music and works written by themselves. In ordinary classes I divided the pupils into small groups, where each group composed small music-theatre works: words and music had to be written out, so that other singers and instrumentalists in the group could read and perform accurately. By year three the classes could sight-sing simple unaccompanied works in three parts.

All this would have been impossible had I not been supported by the county education authority in Gloucester, who provided free of charge the instruments for the orchestra, and tuition for the children by peripatetic teachers. A more 'popular' musical culture flourished in the school, too – it is both musically and spiritually demanding to improvise jazz, play pop-music by ear, and to invent pop-style songs about the traumas of adolescence. The standard of work in other subjects was thought to be helped by all this music-making, which not only encouraged the mental and physical skills of playing and singing together but, perhaps just as significant, helped the children's social skills.

Had I not served my time as a school music teacher, I would not have been the composer of *Eight Songs for a Mad King* and other music-theatre works. I learned more about liberation through music from the Cirencester children than they ever learned from me – or than I learnt from specialist new-music festivals like Darmstadt or Donaueschingen.

It followed that groups of these children could perform standard repertoire, works specially written for them, and music by the children themselves. We went to the Bath and Cheltenham Festivals and to the Royal Festival Hall in London, with radio and television broadcasts. When taken to concerts of old or new music as audience these young people made informed listeners, with stimulating arguments in the bus home afterwards.

In Cirencester, music was a healing and binding element, both in the school, and in the town – just as it is now in the community on the island of Sanday, Orkney, where I live, with its fiddle group and chorus, and on the mainland of Orkney with its many musical outlets.

It is not only the cuts in music education in state schools which are responsible for the lack of interest in classical music among young people, aware of concerts where the heads of listeners are often mainly grey and white. It is also due to the relentless peer pressure put upon young people to conform – to like the latest pop group, clothes, haircut, TV lore, or street language to define clan membership. Outside interests may be derided. This demands some further consideration of the aims of our education system, in relation to society as a whole, and to the place of music within this framework.

What happens at school or college is only a part of the story: the main influence on most people's lives now is television. With a huge choice of commercial channels, the lowest common denominator prevails, so that the best efforts of channels with the remnants of public service ethics – informing, educating, and entertaining – are swamped in a sea of dross. It may also be indicative that many television programmes, even serious documentaries, left with a space between words, pump out mindless, brittle *muzak*, demonstrating the programme-makers' lack of faith in our powers of concentration, and trivialising any visuals. Freedom in broadcasting has come to mean scrapping quality and maximising advertising takings by providing programmes for people who 'know what they like'. You only know what you like when you can make an informed choice, and our education system hardly provides for that. Circulation figures for the popular papers in comparison with their so-called highbrow stable-mates show that most people leave school with a restricted vocabulary and that their thinking is thereby severely limited. Issues are now stated in oversimplified terms, determined by popular-press vocabulary and the attention span of a television commercial sound-bite. Perhaps not only our children, but all of us are being educated to become docile consumers. We become incapable, or perhaps just unwilling, through pressures, to question the status quo: the drug to perpetuate this is television – which is now the opium of the people – helped and underwritten by an education system which fails to challenge all its implied commercial values.

Until recently anybody interested in music could have borrowed scores from a public library. If you are lucky now, you can pick up bargains as these sell off their musical collections to fill the shelves with more 'relevant' material that will be borrowed more often. At this rate, there could come a time when libraries will stock only textbooks, self-help DIY texts, and Mills & Boon. Studying a musical score online is a poor substitute for handling a printed one, and buying new scores is prohibitively expensive. When I was a boy, browsing the music shelves in Swinton and Pendlebury public libraries was a formative experience which determined my career – and I bet I was the only one to borrow some of that music. Was it worth it? Obviously not by today's values.

While classical music may be experiencing some difficulties in the concert hall, the availability of music on the web is perhaps a positive development. I have a website from which anyone with a computer and credit card can download a sequence of my works, with relevant programme notes elegantly provided, or order up a CD to be sent through the post. The response is most encouraging, from all over the world – at least there are people out there wanting to listen, with sufficient numbers to stimulate further investment in new titles.

In London there are the BBC Symphony and four other main orchestras, along with other professional chamber orchestras and groups, seeking to fill, night after night, the South Bank, the Barbican and the Royal Albert Hall. Taking their lead from pioneering work done by Kathryn McDowell, Ian Ritchie and the Scottish Chamber Orchestra in the nineteen eighties, all these orchestras, along with opera houses and groups like the London Sinfonietta, have their 'outreach' programmes. In Scotland I was commissioned by the Strathclyde Regional Council and the Scottish Arts Council to write ten *Strathclyde Concertos* for the Scottish Chamber Orchestra featuring their principal players. With each concerto there was an accompanying outreach/educational programme, whereby a young composer – James MacMillan, Sally Beamish, Ian McQueen, Alasdair Nicholson and others – would encourage children in selected Strathclyde schools to compose and perform, with members of the SCO, new works whose kicking-off point was the particular *Strathclyde Concerto* I had just composed. Just before the first performance of my new work, all the participating children would meet up to play and hear their own new works. Then, finally, the children would come to the concert to hear the first performance, in Glasgow City Hall, of my own new piece. I remember a group of girls after the first performance of my Cello Concerto saying how much they enjoyed my music, but wasn't that other thing I conducted – a Schubert Symphony, as it happened – a bore! I realised that we had done part of our work well enough. The difficulty about these outreach/educational programmes is their transitory nature. The schools usually have just one term's follow-up, and without a background of literate musical education, the value of the exercise is diminished.

I am aware that even in some respected bastions of musical education the knowledge of music notation is regarded as élitist, that classical music itself is élitist. In the sense that a little prior study and knowledge helps towards listening and participation, of course it is just that, along with any other field such as science, literature or football. It is only in music that these inverted snobs take this line. These people would deny the likes of me, a working-class boy from Salford, access to some of the most wonderful things in our civilisation. I will always fight for them to be available to all, even to the lower-paid and to the underprivileged. However, with successive governments demonstrating a lack of concern for cultural standards, particularly in education, it is hardly surprising that orchestras, museums and theatres should be forever struggling, strapped for cash.

One can hardly blame the schoolteachers. In my time there have been at least four complete overhauls of the school curriculum with many directives for change. With insufficient discussion with the teachers, who have to implement these directives, it is surprising that, even if often bewildered and a little confused, they remain cheerful and positive. Moreover, with teacher training time now inadequate to prepare teachers for what they must face in the classroom, it is hardly astonishing that music has fared badly. It is a waste of human resources that some teachers have to be more concerned with keeping order among their mutinous and resentful charges, than opening doors to any kind of life-enhancing cultural opportunities.

In 2004 the government produced *The Music Manifesto: More Music for More People*.[2] This was a splendid, very political document, full of promise, but without mention of dates for implementation of proposals, or mention of practical resources. For example: 'we believe that over time, every primary school child should have opportunities for sustained and progressive instrumental tuition, offered free of charge or at a reduced rate'. 'Over time' is blurred indeed, and no mention is made of when it could happen in relation to an already full timetable, who will foot the bill, and who will cope with head teachers who see such things as useless, decorative frills. 'Every child should have access to a wide range of high quality live music experiences and a sound foundation in general musicianship ... We will promote effective curriculum delivery for music throughout secondary schools', and so on – all most worthy if there is practical follow-up of these good intentions.

In some schools there is great satisfaction because computers are available, upon which the pupils can compose music. Harmony, of a kind, can be added automatically, as well as rhythmic backing tracks. Each student works away with personal headphones, alone in a tight little musical world, and everyone is very proud of the technological achievement, and of the production of original musical composition.

Music is, or was, a social activity. You composed it for, and rehearsed and performed it with, friends and colleagues. Here, in a world where already so much of life is spent in computer isolation, music becomes yet another solitary occupation. For exams pupils are required to produce not only original compositions, but exercises in harmony. These can be done on the computer, and the machine can check for errors, such as parallel perfect fifths. I am sent unsolicited much new music to consider for conducting with orchestras or, solicited, by the Society for the Promotion of New Music, for possible inclusion in its concerts. It is often dreadfully clear that the music is computer generated, with automatic processes and little guidance from any inner ear, and little awareness of syntax and grammar. I am not

---

2 Department for Education and Skills, *The Music Manifesto: More Music for More People* (Annesley: DfES Publications, 2004), unpaginated.

saying that the computer cannot be used creatively for composition and notation with imagination and flair, but it cannot substitute for thought processes. Technology can be a wondrous aid, but it cannot take over and direct.

Once in a tertiary music college or a university music department, a composition student pursues a practical and academic course, with the occasional opportunity to hear a work rehearsed and performed, usually by fellow students, and occasionally by professionals. But practical experience is normally limited, and at the end of three or four years a student receives a paper qualification as a composer, but with not enough worldly know-how. Far better, I think, would be an apprentice scheme, whereby, under the watchful eye and ear of someone experienced in each field, a promising young composer could be lent to a local choral society, brass band, primary or secondary school, television or radio station, as well as professional and amateur orchestras, chamber music societies, and drama groups. I find it distressing that, when a new work is in rehearsal at, say, Covent Garden or the Royal Festival Hall, there are very seldom composition students there learning the ropes, getting the feel of the situation before they experience their own rehearsals under these circumstances. It is this lack of practical experience among many later twentieth-century composers which, along with the arcane nature of much of their music, so alienated musicians. I am not advocating that a composer should compromise his or her inspiration – just that one should work, as far as possible, with a practical knowledge of any difficulties in the work when that moment of baffled confrontation occurs in rehearsal.

However, I must be careful in what I say – conductors and members of orchestras used to accuse me of exactly this lack of practical knowledge. I remember in 1965, for the sake of a quiet life, rescoring a long passage where the trumpets of a professional London orchestra claimed that what I had written was impossible. Ten years before, I had written a sonata for trumpet and piano for Elgar Howarth and John Ogdon, where the trumpet part was much more difficult, and which every trumpet student is expected to play today. These days the said orchestral passage is sight-read without difficulty or comment, which makes me quietly smile – I hope not too smugly.

In 2004, to my utter astonishment, I was offered the position of Master of the Queen's Music. The brief was to raise the profile of serious music, and providing music for Royal occasions was entirely optional. I accepted, in a spirit of optimism and idealism. I know there are some who questioned my integrity, and found it difficult to reconcile my *enfant terrible* reputation from the 1960s with becoming now such an establishment figure. I have always accepted jobs where the territory was new to me, such as writing film music for Ken Russell, or a work for the Boston Pops. This new position posed problems I had never faced to do with communicating with large, non-new-music-specialist audiences, under unfamiliar conditions. I believed that, if new classical music was to succeed in the twenty-first century, I could help, in a minor way, to contribute to that future. On 6 June 2005 I conducted *Commemoration '45*, at a Royal Concert of Reconciliation in Central Hall, Westminster. This twenty-minute work was a Royal Commission jointly with the Royal British Legion and the Royal Philharmonic Orchestra, to commemorate the sixtieth anniversary of the ending of World War II. It brought together the combined forces of the London Symphony Chorus, the Royal Philharmonic Orchestra, the Central Band of the Royal British Legion, the trumpets of the Royal Military School of Music, Kneller Hall, and the boys of the choirs of St Paul's Cathedral, Westminster Abbey, Westminster Cathedral, and the Chapel Royal, Hampton Court. This was my own initiative, done without compromise, and I was happy to learn from works like Britten's *War Requiem* and pieces by Prokofiev and Shostakovich, to help me pitch it right.

I saw it as part of my new job to become involved with Kneller Hall and the Royal British Legion. I have never been an absolute pacifist, realising that, but for the armed services between 1939 and 1945, I would not be here. It was absolutely necessary to fight Hitler. However, I am well aware that, for the first time in history, the British armed forces were hijacked on behalf of a foreign, possibly illegal, fundamental-religious neo-colonial crusade. Under these circumstances it is important to me that I signal not only understanding of the predicament and moral dilemma faced by the military, but that I actively support those involved in military music in the most practical way. The Queen herself is a Head of State, outside politics, for whom I can work openly and honestly, while making known, as a private citizen, what I see as a betrayal of democratic principle.

I am also involved with Westminster Abbey and the Chapel Royal. While standing well outside orthodox religion, I have written two complete masses. As the authorities at Westminster Cathedral said, when they commissioned a Pentecostal Mass from me, they had commissioned Britten, and he was not a Catholic, and they had commissioned Vaughan Williams, who was an atheist – it is the music which is of interest. I have always found religion fascinating, though I respect contemporary secular intelligence and curiosity more. I have read Aquinas, Boethius, Augustine, and Donne, and found the buildings and artworks expressing Christianity, loaded with symbolism and complex iconography, an inspiration. While understanding that religion is there to help us come to terms with our mortality, I have thus far never felt the need, and what the faithful assure us happens to us after death is so speculative that I have not become involved. St Augustine wrote: Fides est virtus qua creduntur quae non videntur. Nos quidquid illud significant faciamus, et quam sit verum, non laboremus. (Faith is a means by which those things that are not seen may be believed; and we may believe whatever it signifies to us, not troubling as to how true such things might be.) I am quite happy to look around, and think that after death I shall be part of that. I do not know what it means, but it implies something which, occasionally, through the music I am writing, becomes almost tangible – but for me words will probably always fail. Occasionally the preoccupation with a personal salvation and everlasting life can seem exaggeratedly self-preoccupied and hubristic. For me religion remains a wonderful work of art.

Perhaps religion has this in common with great art: it is not there primarily to offer comfort, but – *pace* King Lear – to make manifest 'the mystery of things'. Both religion and art make us aware of the deepest questions at the heart of things, as, indeed, does science. This is precisely the attraction of classical music. It takes time to work its magic, needing time to unfold in performance, time spent in preparation, and time for first impressions to sink in and mature. This puts its survival in a world of instant coffee, junk food and the sound-bite, under some duress; and, because a symphony or an oratorio is an expensive minority interest, it cannot usually be exploited for profit. It can only survive because it is considered of cultural significance, and a part of the essential fabric of our civilisation.

Particularly in Austria, classical music is an integral part of life. The British ambassador in Vienna is not only fluent in German, but has a music degree from Oxford and participates as a cellist in chamber music. When I, as a classical composer, visit Austria professionally, there are television cameras at the airport and interviews for the main TV news. I mention this not from hubris, but to point out that such a thing is inconceivable in Britain, except for pop stars. There are reasons. In Austria classical music has been composed for hundreds of years, and people are proud of it. At last year's Carinthian Summer Festival I gave the keynote speech at the opening ceremony. The Prime Minster should have been there, but he had recently died; his acting deputy sent a message. But something of Austria's cultural vigour, and belief in classical music for all, in particular for the young, was brought home to me at a performance, in the full main theatre of Villach, of three of the children's music-theatre works I have written for Orkney schools over the past twenty years. Five hundred or so schoolchildren took part on stage and in the orchestra pit in excellent performances. I have never experienced anything quite on that scale in Britain.

In the first Elizabeth age, as well as before, we in England had a musical culture second to none in Europe. In the seventeenth century Purcell was as brilliant a star as any in the firmament. At the time of Bach we had a German import – Handel. But through the times of Haydn, Mozart, Beethoven and into the nineteenth century, the musical scene here was of less interest. With the late-nineteenth-century renaissance of British music, above all with Elgar, and into the twentieth century with Holst, Vaughan Williams, Britten and that whole pantheon, we can hold our heads high. I would insist that today we are producing not only performing musicians as good as any in the world, but some of the most accomplished and distinguished composers. However, when I conduct orchestras in Europe, there are always ex-pat Brits there because there was no job for them in Britain, or because conditions and salaries in other countries are so much better than here. We have five opera houses, Germany has over ninety, and comparison in the orchestral field is similar. In Germany the artistic community has been complaining bitterly about government cuts, but in comparison with Britain, they are still in clover.

The roots of a thriving classical music scene need three nutrients, of which the first is music education, and the second, resources. However, this is perhaps a poor proposition for a government wishing to be perceived as prudent with taxpayers' money, and where the private sector, though taking a real interest, still has no tax incentive to contribute. The third nutrient is new music. Classical music cannot become a museum culture, however tempting for some such a proposition may be. All performers, to be really alive, must be in a constructive relationship with contemporary culture, and this means live composers. The composer-in-residence schemes of some orchestras are splendid, and I warmly welcomed the announcement of the Royal Philharmonic Society's Composer in the House scheme. I benefited from such arrangements with the Scottish Chamber Orchestra, the Royal Philharmonic and the BBC Philharmonic. In writing numerous works for their players, and conducting concerts with all kinds of repertoire, I learned so much from the musicians involved. I would recommend all composers to grasp any such opportunity. Perhaps it seems daunting, as an inexperienced conductor, to stand in front of such a group of players, but if you have prepared well and are honest, its members will do all they can to help and make the performances work.

The present and past British governments' attitudes to our cultural heritage have been bizarre enough, and I do not wish to make unfair comparisons, but I would like to quote, as a warning of how bad things could get, Moshe Lewin on the post-Soviet attitude to these things in the new Russia: 'Not content with looting and squandering the nation's wealth, the "reformers" mounted a frontal assault on the past, directed at its culture, identity and vitality. This was no critical approach to the past, it was sheer ignorance.'[3] I think we should at least be warned.

Classical music is such an integral part of European culture that it should be regarded as something available to all by right. It no longer occupies central attention in our musical world – many other kinds of music are, quite rightly, up there with it. I pointed out that the masterpieces of classical music are the sound equivalents of the great cathedrals, and I trust nobody is thinking of leaving them to rot.

'Aemulamini autem charismata meliora' (But be ye zealous for the

---

3 Moshe Lewin, *The Soviet Century*, ed. Gregory Elliott (London: Verso, 2005).

better gifts).[4] When our very existence is threatened by climate change, we can only strive and hope that civilised institutions can continue. I would love to spend more time performing, to dedicate more attention to music education at all levels, and even to do what I think of as agitprop for classical music, but the demon that drives me is musical composition, and unless I spend most of my time involved in that, I feel I am not fulfilling my role as a creative human being. *Sub specie aeternitatis*, this is a very small matter, but, thinking again of the *St Matthew Passion*, perhaps it was not always so small, and could even be not such a small matter again. I believe that classical music has a future, assuming we, as a civilised society, have any prospects at all. However, one must never forget that, not far into the seventeenth century, when, with Shakespeare and Marlowe, we had the best theatre in the world, it was all destroyed by an unsympathetic government, under the influence of what we would today call the religious right.

4 1 Corinthians 12:31.

# PART III

# A 2013 PERSPECTIVE

# What Happened to the Music?

JOHN STEPHENS

THE FIVE BERNARR RAINBOW LECTURES span a decade from the
first, delivered by Baroness Warnock in October 1999, to the last,
given in May 2010 by Professor Gavin Henderson. Drawing on his own
considerable experience in music and the arts, Henderson's 'Reflections
and Progressions' relate to notions of improvement: every new initiative is
an upgrade.

Progress can imply change, but whether or not it is an improvement
upon what went before is dependent upon individual values and
philosophy, opportunities and, not least, resources. Many today who are
committed to the fundamental rationale for music education, as set out in
the Lectures, would find it hard to see progress as new structures emerge
and resources markedly decrease. The halcyon days of music education
may be seen through rose-coloured spectacles, yet some aspects of the
current scene provide new and possibly more effective ways to achieve the
universal goals in music education as articulated by the five lecturers, along
with Sir Peter Maxwell Davies in his 2005 Royal Philharmonic Society
Lecture.

The lecturers, and Rainbow himself, recognised an uneven provision
for music from school to school and an overloaded curriculum in state
schools. Concerns about all subjects were expressed by Prime Minister
James Callaghan in 1976.[1] This openly criticised the education system and
signalled a political intention to have national standards of performance
in state schools with the objective of 'better preparing a workforce for
industry and business'. This rationale was a watershed for music and
the arts whose justification was strongly related to developing creativity,
imagination and a civilising influence in society. It was over a decade

1 The Prime Minister discussed education in a landmark speech at the ceremony for
laying the foundation-stone of Ruskin College, Oxford, on 18 October 1976; full text
in *The Guardian* 15 October 2001; see also Andrew Adonis, *The Guardian*, 17 October
2006.

later that, in the Education Reform Act of 1988, legislation was passed to introduce a National Curriculum for schools, and music became a statutory requirement for Key Stages one, two and three (taken between five and fourteen years old).

The millennium has seen political influence on schools exercised first through the curriculum, second through the control of resources, and third directly in their management and organisation. The National Curriculum provided the framework for teaching and assessing pupils' progress, whilst restructuring the distribution of resources to schools placed additional responsibilities on head teachers and governors. 'Local Management of Schools' (LMS), as it was titled, took schools out of direct financial control of their local authority; the far-reaching implications are explored later in this paper.

The effects of the first, a National Curriculum, were largely positive for music that was accorded status as one of its ten subjects. Publishers and instrument suppliers produced a flurry of materials and approaches to music activities in the classroom, often carefully graded to match the targets children were given to achieve at the end of each Key Stage. Assessing pupils' progress in music became a focus for debate and discussion. As the assessments of pupils' progress and development against the standards (Attainment Targets) set by the National Curriculum were undertaken, the debate within the whole arts-education community centred upon what was assessable, and what was not. Alongside the impetus given to music education by its inclusion in the National Curriculum, there was also a marked decline in providing opportunities for pupils to develop their imagination, opportunities so strongly promoted by John Paynter and Baroness Warnock: the emphasis was on the assessment-led curriculum.

There were other issues of general concern across many, if not all, subjects in the curriculum. The transition from primary to secondary school was signalled as a potentially weak process: often the secondary schools, receiving pupils from many and varied primary schools, assumed that pupils had no experience of music at all. There was a feeling of starting from the beginning all over again, with secondary schools ignoring what had been taught at primary level. There was clearly a need for closer understanding to ensure continuity of pupils' learning; locally, various schemes were launched to strengthen the links between the stages of education, including secondary music specialists visiting and teaching in their feeder primary schools. The nature of musical activity, involving different skill levels, seems ideally suited to such collaboration. Schools' music festivals sustain this in some places.

Concerned about the poor state of children's literacy, David Blunkett, Education Secretary in 1998, introduced what became known as the 'literacy hour': at least one hour a day for all primary school pupils, to be spent on phonics, spelling and grammar. Schools had become the very centre of political control, and a schools' inspection regime mounted by the Office of Standards in Education (OFSTED) was set to ensure compliance. With a fifth of school-time spent on the literacy hour, schools adjusted the time allocated for other subjects, and music suffered. There was a wide perception that music education, with opportunities to learn an instrument, was in decline.

Music activities make ideal showcases for schools to demonstrate participating offspring to their parents; nativity plays, carol services, choirs, bands and orchestras all played a part in promoting schools that were often in competition with each other to attract pupils. Few other school subjects have the same level of promotional appeal and entertainment value. Thus, when declining funds for instrumental music tuition was added to the reduced time allocated for music on the timetable, music educators found that they had a strong army of campaigners: parents are also voters, as politicians knew. Add the influence of some notable professional musicians, including Simon Rattle and Peter Maxwell Davies, and a very powerful lobby emerged. It is worthy of note that music educators have long enjoyed the support of professional musicians; few if any other curriculum subjects are so endorsed in this way.

Henderson's lecture recounts an anecdote that is relevant here: he recognised David Blunkett over his garden wall in Brighton. As Education Secretary at the time, Blunkett stemmed the growing criticism of school music with the statement that he believed that 'every child should have the chance to learn an instrument'. Of course, it may have been a throw-away political line, but the music-education community seized upon it as salvation. From the start it was clear that the resource implications of Blunkett's line had just not been considered. Were there sufficient instrumental teachers to deliver the undertaking? Were instruments available, and what instruments were to be offered? These and other questions raised by Blunkett's statement eventually led to its refinement: 'over time, all pupils in primary schools who wish to, will have the opportunity to learn a musical instrument'. While his promise has never been fulfilled, it led to a shift in the methodology for instrumental music tuition.

Blunkett backed his statement with increased resources, using an existing development fund in his department, the Standards Fund, for which local Music Services could apply. Patterns of provision for what became known as 'Wider Opportunities' varied throughout the country; they were dependent upon the management skill of the heads of Music Services and the number and quality of teachers available. Broadly it enabled primary school pupils to receive instrumental music lessons as part of a group, often the whole class.

The traditional pattern of one-to-one tuition, copied from conservatoire and private teaching methods, gave way to larger groups or even whole classes for beginners. Lessons for one or two terms, possibly a whole year in some areas, were described as a foundation; thereafter parents, or in some cases schools, met the costs. Instruments were supplied through the scheme. Most Music Services grasped the new challenge – training the staff and, as far as possible, delivering on Blunkett's pledge. The pace of change required quick adaptation to meet the politically generated criteria for funding, and whilst many succeeded, some teachers found Wider Opportunities beyond their reach. Group teaching of instruments has a long pedigree: Suzuki, Paul Roland, Yvonne Enoch and many others have all, in their time, developed schemes that exploit the value of having more than one learner in the classroom, especially for the beginner stages. In some areas adaptations were made to the scheme, but what few saw at the time was that public funds, previously used to support all stages of proficiency from beginner through to well beyond grade eight for some, were being redirected and deployed almost exclusively for the beginner stage. For some instrumental teachers this meant a continuous diet of teaching beginners.

With public funding used in this way, schools and parents were left to meet the costs for pupils who wished, and were sufficiently committed, to continue. As schools met the challenge of allocating priorities for subjects within the school timetable of twenty-five hours a week, many substituted these instrumental music lessons under the Wider Opportunities scheme for the music lessons in the classroom. This strategy was reinforced by the lack of skill and confidence of many primary school teachers to teach music.

It may never be known if a more planned and gradual introduction of group tuition, with the opportunity to give teachers a secure training, would have saved the national scheme; doubtless some influences will have rubbed off and some may soldier on, but Blunkett's big dream has all but evaporated. Politicians can have a strategic influence on the curriculum but their relatively short life expectancy in power gives insufficient time for new and maybe worthwhile approaches to take root in the curriculum. The influence of Paynter and others, backed by solid academic institutions, has proved of greater lasting benefit to music education than have even the most noble of political initiatives.

A vision for 'what might be' has been replaced by structures for 'formula funding', and there is little expectation of long-term public funding to develop musical talent in schools. As resources for public spending have been reduced, the distribution of funds to Music Services has now been transferred from the government's Education Department to the Arts Council.

Funding has always been pluralist, as Lord Moser observed in his lecture of 2000. Government, local authorities, parents and other patrons have all supported the financing of music education; it is the balance and control that fluctuates within the political and economic climate. The 1988 Education Act, introduced by Education Secretary Kenneth Baker, gave individual schools greater control of the available public funds for education. With these resources schools could 'buy in' the services – materials and teachers – that they required. Of course larger schools had bigger budgets and that gave them greater flexibility in deploying resources. While there was a transition period in which some local authorities maintained and fully funded a Music Service, gradually music instrumental tuition became a service that schools could purchase, choosing whether or not to pass on the costs, in full or part, to parents.

As Music Services became businesses, those who headed them quickly found themselves in need of skills to manage and run them. The focus for their activity moved from methodology, repertoire and the curriculum, to contracts, budgets and conditions of employment. The livelihood of the teachers within each Music Service often rested upon the capacity of the Heads of Service to market and maintain the expected quality of service that had once been delivered through the local authority, free, to the classroom door.

Baroness Warnock recognised the importance of singing being a 'regular element' in children's education. School morning assemblies, in which hymn-singing was a daily activity, belong to a generation now well past the school gates. A gradual decline in singing in schools has been noted over the years: playing instruments and electronic keyboards appear to have become priority activities in music lessons. The use of sophisticated sound technology, notably in popular culture, has been reflected in schools' extending its use through to A-level examination with the introduction of Music Technology as an additional subject alongside Music. Curiously the teenagers, familiar with electro-acoustic sounds of popular vocal culture, seemed uninterested in singing themselves. There were distinguished exceptions with some choral ensembles achieving high standards, as for example the notable National Youth Choir, but singing was not securely bedded into the school music curriculum.

Being persuaded of the need to halt this decline, the government of the day appointed Howard Goodall as National Singing Ambassador and injected £50m over five years into a national singing initiative, Sing Up, with the aim of putting singing at the heart of every primary school. Thus, as with the Wider Opportunities initiative, public funds came directly from government rather than school budgets.

Inspired by the remarkable results of the programme of music and social education in Venezuela known as El Sistema, in 2009 the UK government launched three pilot projects in England to 'use music to bring positive change to the lives of children in disadvantaged areas'; a similar initiative was also promoted in Scotland. The programme, broadly based on the principles of El Sistema, aimed to encourage participation through large ensembles of symphonic proportions in classical music. Established now as a charitable organisation, In Harmony currently supports five projects across England with public funds assured until 2015.

The visible, indeed audible, success of the nearly forty-year-old scheme of the Venezuelan National Network of Youth and Children's Orchestras is in the 125 youth orchestras it maintains with government funding, the now world-famous Símon Bolívar Symphony Orchestra, and its conductor Gustavo Dudamel, himself a product of the scheme and currently Music Director of the Los Angeles Philharmonic Orchestra. The publicity afforded in this country to this remarkable achievement seemingly overlooks the accomplishments at home, such as that of the National Youth Orchestra of Great Britain, where the talents of many aspiring young professional musicians have been nurtured, including those of Simon Rattle, the current conductor of the Berliner Philharmoniker, one of the world's greatest orchestras.

Commendable as the In Harmony initiative in England has been, it does not address fundamental weaknesses in the uneven patterns of provision for music education as identified by Warnock and Moser in their lectures. Politicians usually seek a high profile and publicity for the projects that they initiate with public funds; however, additional public funds for uncoordinated projects does not necessarily lead to the upgrade being sought by music educators.

Alongside the transformation of Music Services, the schools themselves were subjected to re-organisation within the tussle for control between central and local government. First, City Technical Colleges, and then Academies and Free Schools (free from local-authority control, that is) were created, and permitted to opt out of direct financial control by local authorities. Whilst the school inspection programme remained in place, and league tables of schools' record of public examination results were published, these 'opted out' schools could also move away from the prescriptions of the National Curriculum and even employ teachers without a training qualification. Deregulation on a massive scale.

The ten-year span of the Bernarr Rainbow Lectures encompassed a major period of change to public education, and this has had many consequences for music educators who, through their various professional bodies, developed considerable skill and influence in lobbying politicians. These bodies, brought together within the Music Education Council, represent sectional and specialised interests, each with its own cohort of supporters displaying the zeal and energy of expert missionaries.

Successive governments did attempt to listen to often divergent views on music education being expressed from numerous vested interests. Seeking to bring together these various stands, David Milliband as Secretary of State for Education initiated a series of conferences for music educators and in October 2004 published a *Music Manifesto* that sought to bring coherence and a greater level of collaboration between the various specialist-interest groups among music educators. The *Manifesto* was a bold statement and, whilst omitting any reference to funding and resources, its visions and dreams had few contentious issues. Organisations with interests in music education were invited to sign the declaration. Most did. Among the signatories were professional bodies – orchestras and opera companies, most of whom had, for many years, been developing their work in schools and the community. Collaboration between schools and professional musicians was not new: for generations musicians have been performing for and with schoolchildren and writing music specially for them. The scale of partnership and the commitment on both sides marked out many of the projects, such as those undertaken through the London Symphony Orchestra's Discovery programme, first established in 1992.

The *Music Manifesto* was a symbol that the government had assumed the role of coordinator of the many and various interests in music education, formerly undertaken by the Music Education Council and its 1960s predecessor, the UK Council for Music Education. While music educators were mostly content to see this happen, their prime reason for dealing with civil servants and ministers was to secure a long-term commitment of public funding resources. No government could provide such an undertaking: HM Treasury Spending Reviews control the flow of public funds to every spending department.

One, possibly little noticed, outcome of the *Music Manifesto* was a closer collaboration over music education matters between the government departments with responsibility for education and the arts. The significance of this dual approach may reach well into the future, but it was noted and acted upon by Michael Gove, the incoming Secretary of State in 2010. Serving a new government committed to cutting public spending in the wake of economic decline, he joined with his colleague Ed Vaizey, Minister for Culture, Communications and Creative Industries, to commission Darren Henley, Managing Director of

Classic FM radio station, to produce 'the first ever national plan for music education'.[2]

*The Importance of Music*, the much-heralded and several-times-delayed report which ensued, reassembled most of Blunkett and Milliband's sentiments of earlier government productions, while confirming reductions in expenditure in all but the In Harmony project.[3] Seeing the diversity of interest-groups in music education, Henley developed the concept of 'hubs' to deliver music education in partnership, building on the work of local-authority Music Services and schools' collaborations with the music profession. The report also had much to commend, and doubtless its positive approach softened the blow of impending cuts. Developing 'hubs' to facilitate partnerships and ensure greater coherence of provision in an area; an ambition for every child to learn a musical instrument; and improving the qualification of those concerned with music education were proposals that were mostly well received. However, the distribution of funds for Music Services was transferred from the Department for Education to the Arts Council England, requiring an additional layer of bureaucracy within an elaborate bidding process.

The move from collaboration to transfer of responsibilities between government departments should be closely monitored by music educators who have long appreciated their discipline's being embraced within the mainstream objectives of the school curriculum. The apparent unwillingness of the current Secretary of State for Education to incorporate arts subjects into his newly designed examination, the English Baccalaureate, to replace GCSE examinations, is a strong indication of a view of the school curriculum that is highly functional and, if implemented, would downgrade music activities in many secondary schools. Ministers in Wales and Northern Island have been critical of a lack of consultation in the proposed changes and it is possible that this may lead to a greater level of diversity of provision throughout the United Kingdom. Whilst opportunities for greater links between music educators and their

2 Henley's initial review was published as *Music in Education in England: A Review by Darren Henley for the Department for Education and the Department for Culture, Media and Sport* (London: DfE and DCMS, 2011).

3 DfE and DCMS, *The Importance of Music: A National Plan for Music Education* (London: DfE and DCMS, 2011).

professional music colleagues and the music industry will doubtless be encouraged through Arts Council England, the transfer of responsibilities should not be a demotion from a major government concern to a relatively low-spending, minor player in the political scene.

The quality and effectiveness of the leadership of hubs will determine their level of success in delivery of the National Music Plan. Even well-run Music Services are likely to find the level of responsibility of hub leadership very demanding, and partnership with schools will be critical, given that head teachers and governors have responsibility for the curriculum whilst the hub leader will be required to 'ensure that every child 5 to 18 learns a musical instrument', upon which government funding is dependent.[4]

The severe reductions in the level of government funding over the years from 2011 to 2014, from £82.5m to £58m, will restrict the scope of provision, yet *The Importance of Music* offers little comment on how its objectives might be achieved within this constraint and there is no guarantee that local authorities will be in a position to continue their funding levels. Apart from a hope to 'draw in and align funding streams from other sources', the report carefully avoids addressing key issues of public funding for music education.[5]

A stimulus for musical activity is to be found in the new opportunities afforded to professional musicians of all genres to engage with the learners of tomorrow through a partnership – educator and musician. Future generations of music educators may well look back at the first decade of the millennium and see a shift of emphasis from curriculum matters – teaching and learning, repertoire and technique – to a preoccupation with systems and structures; from developing the imagination and creativity to meeting prescribed targets. In other words, moving further away from the music itself. If a lesson is to be learnt from the last decade it surely must be: to stay close to the music.

4 DfE and DCMS, *The Importance of Music*, p. 11.

5 DfE and DCMS, *The Importance of Music*, p. 28.

# PART IV

# THREE VIEWS ON MUSIC EDUCATION

In 1994 the Australian Society for Music Education published a symposium in honour of Sir Frank Callaway (1919–2003), the pioneering figure in music education on the international scene: *Music Education: International Viewpoints: A Symposium in Honour of Emeritus Professor Sir Frank Callaway*, ed. Martin Comte, ASME Monograph Series 3 (Nedlands, Western Australia: Australian Society for Music Education, 1994). The three contributions from that symposium included here originally appeared as Bernarr Rainbow, 'Music Education, Yesterday, Today and Tomorrow: A British Perspective', pp. 153–9; John Paynter, 'Keeping Music Musical: A British Perspective', pp. 143–6; and Wilfrid Mellers, 'A British Perspective', pp. 121–5. They are reprinted by permission of the editor.

# Music Education, Yesterday, Today and Tomorrow

BERNARR RAINBOW

CONTRARY TO COMMON OPINION, reminiscence over a long life does not automatically mean thinking that nothing now is as good as it used to be; and that everything – music education included – has gone to the dogs. Once unshakeable Victorian belief in the inevitability of human progress may have received a battering during the past century's disasters. But in the field of music education at least, remarkable progress has clearly been made since music lessons were reintroduced into the generality of English schools during the nineteenth century. However, that does not mean that perfection has been reached – and the future can be seen to hold both opportunities and weighty challenges ...

My own clear memory of the very modest music lessons typical of the London elementary schools I attended early in the 1920s is of singing by rote 'Early One Morning', 'Come, lasses and lads', 'Hearts of Oak', and other by now defunct items from the ubiquitous *National Song Book*.[1] The rest of the lesson was spent on sight-reading exercises pointed out by the teacher on a Tonic Sol-fa Modulator slung over the blackboard. All this would take place around the piano in the school hall; otherwise our own class-teachers (invariably non-pianists) produced a tuning fork and 'gave us the note'. There was no other musical equipment or provision; but once a week a mature lady came after school to teach the violin to a handful of children. To emphasise her extra-mural status she always taught wearing an elaborate hat.

At the age of seven or eight I didn't dislike singing those songs – I was already in a church choir – but the sight-reading part bored me and I got into trouble for 'not paying attention'. This I now realise, was because I

---

1 Charles Villiers Stanford (ed. and arr.), *The National Song Book: A Complete Collection of the Folksongs, Carols and Rounds suggested by the Board of Education*, London: Boosey & Co., 1905.

was already learning to play the piano and the names *doh, ray, me* seemed to me both pointless and undignified; meanwhile my less wilful classmates were singing to the teacher's rapidly moving pointer with ease. This shameful recollection incidentally strengthens my belief in the wisdom of introducing ear-sharpening exercises with sol-fa well before instrumental activity begins.

Music lessons at school went on in much the same way for me until I gained a scholarship at eleven which took me on to a Grammar school.[2] There, as in other boys' (mainly fee-paying) secondary schools those days, we were introduced to the mysteries of Latin, Chemistry, Physics, French, etc.; now Music was not taught at all. However, the private piano lessons my parents paid for were continued, and I started learning to play the organ. At fifteen I had a minimally salaried organ post; but my own reading apart, musical tuition as such did not begin again until I left school. When that time came I enrolled part-time at a London conservatoire and began working for various diplomas.[3] In order to do my Harmony exercises I now found I had to learn to pitch notes mentally – something I could have learnt to do far less arduously at school ten years earlier. But World War II came before long to upset the pattern of life for us all.

My first job on leaving the wartime army was as organist and choirmaster at a large provincial church with a fine musical tradition;[4] with it went a post teaching singing, percussion band, and thirty-six piano pupils a week at a local preparatory school.[5] A few months later I was offered the appointment as music master at the town's Royal Grammar School.[6] Founded in 1562, it is revealing from our point of view to learn that this ancient school had never previously had a full-time music master.

2 Rutlish School, Merton. For further detail about Rainbow's schooling, see *Bernarr Rainbow on Music: Memoirs and Selected Writings*, ed. Peter Dickinson (Woodbridge: Boydell Press, 2010).

3 Trinity College of Music, where Rainbow took the LGSMD (Choir-training and Accompaniment), 1940; ARCM (Music Appreciation and Harmony), 1941; further diplomas followed – LTCL (Class Music Teaching), 1946; LRAM (Choral Conducting), 1950; FTCL (Research in Music), 1961; and, of course, higher degrees.

4 All Saints Parish Church, High Wycombe.

5 Oakend Preparatory School, Gerrards Cross.

6 The Royal Grammar School, High Wycombe (1945–52).

The unclaimed musical desert it represented now became mine to till and sow; and the experience proved limitlessly fulfilling. I took my own record-player and all my 78 rpm discs to school to start off with; and before long every lunch-hour was occupied with junior and senior choirs, a madrigal club, music society, band and embryonic orchestral rehearsals, in addition to an orthodox time-table of class activities.

Meanwhile, with the co-operation of the County Music Adviser (a newly created post in those days) I could draw on the services of sundry peripatetic teachers, enabling suitable boys to take up orchestral instruments. The new 1944 Education Act responsible for that development had also recently recommended a range of musical activities in secondary schools; and I had an enlightened headmaster who supported all these endeavours. Optional 'sets' of boys were now recruited to prepare for external examinations in Music at 'Ordinary', 'Advanced', and 'Scholarship' levels. Even the hitherto sacrosanct Sixth Form was given a music timetable. Music had become respectable!

Looking back half-a-century later on all this, it is still possible to recapture something of the glow of satisfaction that each exhausting day produced; but it would be misleading not to acknowledge that without the boost of the BBC radio music programs, wartime orchestral concerts, and improved gramophone recordings, public and thence parental acceptance of music as a subject worthy of being taught in academically ambitious schools would have been less readily forthcoming.

It was, of course, at that time and also as a result of the 1944 Education Act that suitable school children were able to take up orchestral instruments and later join the regional and national Youth Orchestras responsible for creating a tradition of excellence that survives to this day. And since that time there has been further great expansion in the provision for teaching music in schools. To begin with, increased opportunities (particularly in boys' secondary schools) urgently demanded additional teachers. As a first step schools were invited to recruit suitable musicians locally. But the number of 'natural' teachers available fell far short of need; and steps had to be taken to train others.

For something over a century the training of non-specialist teachers for state schools in Britain had been undertaken in a nationwide chain of colleges. Each was equipped to develop modest levels of competence to teach the standard range of school subjects (including music) to children up to the existing school-leaving age of fourteen. Meanwhile specialist teachers for secondary schools (now to be greatly increased by the raising of school-leaving age) had been recruited from among university graduates and holders of music diplomas.

A disadvantage of this dual system of provision was that while teachers for elementary schools were primed in methods of teaching a group of basic subjects about which they possessed very limited knowledge, teachers for secondary schools who had spent several years studying specialisms received no formal guidance on how to teach them.

Steps taken to remedy this disparity were not perhaps altogether successful; but the number of better-trained graduates and better-educated non-graduates grew as a result. Less happily, however, the efforts of the teacher training colleges to help students with teaching skills were lampooned in some quarters as 'chalk and talk'. Defensively, they now claimed as their overall task, not 'training' teachers, but 'educating' them. Towards that end the academic content of their syllabuses (now including 'Educational Theory') was raised to levels that risked over-stretching at least some of the students involved.

It does not seem to have been generally appreciated at this point that teaching music in schools makes special demands not matched in less practical disciplines. For example, questions of establishing class-discipline apart, while an intelligent tyro well equipped in Geography does not find it too difficult to begin teaching it to a class, a young musician required to pass on something of his own skill and understanding to children faces a much more demanding task.

It will be unnecessary here to stress the problems involved in encouraging pupils to learn to perform and respond to music intelligently. Suffice to say that without considerable guidance in dealing with the techniques involved, young teachers cannot be expected to meet the demands of the classroom realistically. Time in college devoted instead to studying music analysis, composition, style, or any of a host of other technical matters, will not compensate for this lack.

Paradoxically perhaps, it is in the primary schools – where general class-teachers are at least nominally responsible for the content of all lessons – that the damage done by failing to train students to teach music adequately is most apparent. For while it is sometimes argued that 'proper' music teaching should be the prerogative of the secondary schools – where music specialists are available – yet it is in the primary school, while children are at the age of heightened learning ability, that the basic aural and vocal skills on which a sound musical education later depends are best acquired. At that age young children can be seen gaining satisfaction from mastering simple pitch distinctions and rhythmic patterns that would hardly hold the same fascination or educational stimulus for them later. To miss grasping that potential is at least short sighted.

Turning to the secondary schools themselves we find a firm conviction among teachers and authorities alike that 'real' music teaching will begin from scratch for each annual intake at this stage. A secondary school that draws its pupils from a wide area will indeed be hard pressed to find a common standard of musical ability among its hotch-potch of newcomers. It is left with no apparent alternative to starting from scratch. Continuity has already become unattainable – with the result that some children are now bored by having to repeat what they have already learnt while the rest struggle to catch up with them. What is then taught is likely to depend almost entirely on the preferences of the individual teachers concerned.

Compared with the frugal lesson content of the early 1920s when, as we have seen, singing and sight-reading made up the whole, the range of musical activity available in today's schools is prodigious. The first signs of growth came late in the twenties when a few private schools introduced primitive gramophone recordings, or more commonly, pieces played on the piano or pianola, to teach 'active listening'. Other schools gradually adopted the idea. Broadcast 'appreciation' lessons for schools followed. A few years later children's percussion bands, comprising miniature drums, triangles, and cymbals, all playing from rhythm-notation to piano accompaniment, became widespread. Then came the bamboo-pipe movement in which children first made, then played, their own instruments; still later the true recorder became a universal feature in schools.

In addition to all these activities the post-war era was to see a rise of interest in music teaching methods current in other countries. The Eurhythmics of Dalcroze, initially in Switzerland, the Galin–Paris–Chevé Method in France, Orff-Schulwerk in Germany, the Kodály Method in

Hungary, the Justine Ward Method in Holland – each attracted devotees in the UK. Partially understood ideas and snippets from each of those exotic methods were also regularly 'borrowed' and incorporated into existing practice; but what attracted most interest among teachers was the use Carl Orff made of pitched instruments.

As a result there was an incursion of so-called 'classroom' instruments – cheaper commercial versions of Orff's glockenspiels, xylophones, and the like; but Orff's declared policy that instrumental work should supplement, not replace, aural training was conveniently forgotten. Instead, children were now invited to 'read' music purely mechanically – by first identifying the names of notes on the page and then striking appropriately lettered chime-bars. The first essential step – that of equipping the child to 'hear' the notes in the mind before playing them – was ignored. This heresy has been allowed to continue in schools ever since and represents an enduring short-coming in music lessons today.

Other developments that followed in the 1960s included 'Experimental Music in Schools' – a progressive activity to encourage creativity, pioneered earlier in a London school by George Self.[7] Rapidly taken up by disciples and imitators elsewhere, Self's approach introduced simple aleatory compositional techniques allowing pupils to invent and record sound patterns and dramatic effects. Following contemporary practice, these were denoted in graphic notation without recourse to orthodox staff notation. Orff-type classroom instruments were used, augmented by a variety of other sound-producing devices; and when guided by an imaginative teacher stimulating results were possible.

Such innovations apart, perhaps the outstanding event of the 1960s was a negative one: the decline and collapse of class-singing. This catastrophe (as it must now be regarded) was not just the result of the universal adoption of classroom instruments – though many teachers found instrumental work more immediately rewarding than training singers, and that attitude influenced the situation. Nor, as some suggest,

7 George Self developed his experimental techniques at Holloway Comprehensive School and was a member of Rainbow's staff at the College of St Mark and St John during the 1960s. His ground-breaking publications include: *New Sounds in Class: A Contemporary Approach to Music* (London: Universal Edition, 1967), and *Aural Adventure: Lessons in Listening* (London: Novello, 1969).

was the decline simply attributable to the lower age of puberty and the earlier voice-change by now evident among both boys and girls – though this was another contributory factor.

Unquestionably the fundamental cause of the general collapse of class-singing in schools at this time was the coming of the pop group – with its overt appeal to the restive young and its characteristic modelling of a defiantly unformed, harsh singing voice. Fans of the quasi-musical violence it displayed understandably had little time for accepted singing standards.

After the arrival of the Rolling Stones and their equally strident imitators, the majority of teachers found it difficult and eventually impossible to get older school children to take class-singing seriously. In some quarters bleak attempts were made to coax classes to sing by introducing less formal repertory and encouraging a rougher style. Instead of 'Fairest Isle',8 employing the head voice, pupils were offered 'A bicycle built for two', sung rumbustiously.9 Enterprising editors began to compile song books on similarly vulgar lines. Defences (and standards with them) were deliberately lowered – but quite unavailingly. Resistance to class-singing in schools was soon found even among the under-twelves, and except in places where good singing and high musical standards formed part of a prized local tradition, the practice was steadily abandoned.

In any case, as we have seen, alternatives to class-singing were by this time readily available. Technical innovations had also increased the range of musical activities in many schools. At first it was the appearance of the tape-recorder that made possible more 'professional' presentation. Later developments in Information Technology went much further – introducing highly sophisticated electronic devices including keyboards, computers with associated software, and synthesisers. These opened the way for children who lacked formal musical skills (but possessed the modern child's natural feeling for such equipment) to take part, under skilled guidance, in quite elaborate ventures.

Crucial tests of the long term value of such innovative methods still lie

8 From *King Arthur* by Henry Purcell.

9 *Daisy Bell (Bicycle Built for Two)* – a popular song written by Henry Dacre in 1892.

in the future; but the challenges and opportunities thus opened to teachers of music as we approach the next century are already foreseeable.

Future levels of musical attainment in what is for most teachers the largely unexplored field opened by Information Technology are bound to vary from school to school. The number of pupils, the calibre of staff, the availability of resources, the value attaching to local traditions – all these and many other circumstances will decide each school's potential. Yet it is already apparent that uniformity of practice from school to school is unlikely – particularly at secondary level.

In so far as good teaching depends less on what is taught than on the way it is taught, this tendency is unexceptionable. A liberal stance that allows good teachers to be guided by their enthusiasms and to select their own priorities has much to commend it. But if a loosely framed curriculum permits less able teachers to be swamped by alternatives it is time to insist that distinction be firmly drawn between what is optional and what is essential among the resources available.

Currently, influential professional opinion favours a practical rather than theoretical content for all school music programs. On a casual reading, perhaps, that policy appears to mean filling available lesson time with active music-making. Yet such an interpretation overlooks the fact that activity in music is not limited to performance. Learning how to listen and respond to music – as opposed to just hearing it – is very much an active pursuit. So is composing and arranging. In a healthy music syllabus it will therefore not be just the eye or the fingers that receive training; a trained ear is a fundamental necessity for performer and audience alike. Those planning school programmes must take the needs of both into account.

Recognition of the importance of training the ear brings into focus the single curriculum component capable of drawing together all other forms of musical activity in schools. Because it forms an essential ancillary to every aspect of fruitful music teaching, training the ear should form a central core throughout the whole music syllabus – not just at secondary level but from the first term in the primary school.

The importance of introducing aural training by means of ear-sharpening sol-fa at an early age has already been touched upon here. It is not taking place in schools generally at present largely because the majority of today's practising primary-school teachers do not feel competent to deal with the matter. Most of them were at school when class singing was in eclipse. They have never learnt themselves – either as children or as teachers-in-training – to sing from sol-fa; some of them, alas, never even learnt to sing properly.

Attempts have been made by means of in-service training in recent years to remedy this situation; but this has resulted in little more than nibbling at the edges of a nationwide problem. Yet, in the course of one of those attempts an experimental cassette designed to provide self-testing drills in pitch recognition and rhythmic notation was introduced. It proved both popular and effective with the teachers concerned and has since been used equally successfully in many classrooms.[10]

That success suggests that a revival of aural training in primary schools need not rely on uncertain teachers nervously pointing out sight-singing exercises. Instead, appropriate application of Information Technology offers a less hazardous way of dealing with a long-standing problem. Where earlier efforts always failed through the understandable unwillingness of general class teachers to teach what they had never managed to master themselves, if taught to associate sound and symbol discerningly by micro-film, teachers and pupils could quickly learn together.[11]

10 Martin Comte, the editor of *Music Education: International Viewpoint*, added here: 'This cassette was prepared by the Curwen Institute, which Dr Rainbow founded in 1978 to bring John Curwen's teaching principles back to modernised form as *The New Curwen Method*. Details are available in *The New Oxford Companion to Music* (1983) in Dr Rainbow's article on Tonic Sol-fa, under the sub-heading, "The New Curwen Method".' In the article referred to, Rainbow wrote: '*The New Curwen Method* was prepared by Dr W. H. Swinburne and published, after two years' experimental use in schools, in 1980 [*The New Curwen Method*, book 1, Curwen Institute, 1980; book 2, Stainer & Bell, 1981; book 3, Stainer & Bell, 1984]. It follows Curwen by concentrating on training the ear, by introducing the notes of the scale in careful stages, and by using hand signs. But instead of letter notation, the hand signs are themselves used as a preliminary form of notation – the hand being moved up and down against a blackboard staff so as to represent accurately the rise and fall of pitch ... The intention is not to teach sight-singing as an end in itself, but to develop those aural concepts and skills upon which all musical response depends, and without which attempts to teach sight-singing invariably disappoint. Once this has been achieved – with obvious benefit to all aspects of music-making, in and out of the classroom – reading from staff notation follows effortlessly.'

11 Rainbow probably had in mind something like DVD.

No single action would enhance music education as a whole so effectively as the establishing of consistent teaching in the nation's primary schools. It is salutary to note how many of the problems that bedevil music lessons with older children do not exist at the lower age: six- and seven year-olds have no acquired prejudices against singing; they approach acquiring fresh skills with a sense of adventure; their delight at mastering each new challenge is unconcealed. Not to take advantage of that readiness to learn is reprehensible.

# Keeping Music Musical

JOHN PAYNTER

IN 1906 THAT MOST INNOVATIVE OF BRITISH ARCHITECTS, Sir Edwin Lutyens, built his first completely classical country house. His client was a rich Yorkshireman who, understandably, was anxious to see not only that he got value for money but also that he got exactly what he wanted. Touring the unfinished building with the architect, the client was shown the proposed position for a black marble staircase. 'But I don't want a black marble staircase', he said, 'I want an oak one.' 'What a pity', said Lutyens. Some months later they visited the house again and the client was surprised to find the black marble staircase installed. 'I told you I didn't want a black marble staircase', he protested. 'I know', replied Lutyens, 'and do you remember I said: "What a pity"?'[1]

What can explain Lutyens's apparent readiness to ride roughshod over his client's wishes? Was the marble staircase that important? The first Lord Balfour (who, as it happens, was Prime Minister at about the time Lutyens was working on that Yorkshire house) is credited with having said, 'Nothing matters very much, and very few things matter at all.' That might well be a useful maximum for a politician, but for an artist or a musician it won't do: in the work of artists, points of detail do matter – and matter a great deal.

Lutyens's approach to architecture was, in every respect, artistic. Nothing could be left to chance: everything had to be decided. In his concept of a building every distinct part (even the door handles and the kitchen sink) was an essential element which in some way had to be related to the whole, and without which the form would not work. And form is everything.

Art is manifest in art objects; completed forms, not half-completed forms. In the concert hall or from a recording we expect a performance – i.e. something 'formed- through(out)'. Mere 'work in progress' would not

---

1 Mary Lutyens, *Edwin Lutyens, by his Daughter* (London: John Murray, 1980), pp. 67–8.

satisfy anyone. Paintings, poems, sculptures, plays, pieces of music: that is what art is about. Everything else in any way associated with art is either incidental or concerned with the realisation and presentation of those art objects.

What do we learn from this about the role of music in education?

It may look as though the greatest success of music education in our schools over the past thirty or forty years has been the shift in emphasis from children sitting in rows listening to recordings of the classics, or copying from the blackboard notes about dead composers, to children being actively involved with music-making. Surely no one would suggest that that was not an achievement; but it tends to obscure the real achievement, which is that we have established music 'as an education' (to use Keith Swanwick's very telling phrase) by accepting that the essential educative force is experience of music as an art.

John Dewey puzzled his contemporaries by telling them that 'What educates is significant experience' – without being too clear about just what kinds of experience were 'significant'. Was it, perhaps, the arts he had in mind? The finished form of an art object 'signifies'; and art educates by offering us the experience of art objects, not only those made by the people we call Artists (with a capital A!), but also whatever we make for ourselves. That is to say, we are educated by our own enterprise: by the artistic significance of something, however simple, that we have devised, thought about and 'formed-through' (including musical or dramatic performance), that is our own, and which provides for us the satisfaction of having realised it in its wholeness.

It is the wholeness – the sense of 'rightness' in the completed form – which gives what we have made – or, if we're listening or looking, what we have accepted on its own terms – its significance. It is self-sufficient, self-explanatory; it needs no words about it. As Debussy said of music, 'There is no theory. All you have to do is to listen.'

The Lutyens story with which we began highlights two very important features of artistic working. First, the need for conviction: there is no place in art for timidity. To think artistically – musically – is to make a bargain with yourself to produce something which, even if it draws upon other people's ideas, ultimately transfigures them and becomes a 'work' or a 'performance' wholly representative of your own point of view. Courage and a sense of adventure in developing ideas is essential; for, as the jazz trumpeter Miles Davis said, 'Music isn't about standing still and becoming safe.'

Commitment like that may be stimulated by the challenge of 'making, out of the ordinary, something out-of-the-ordinary.' This is universal. Storr points out that Man's quest for integration and unity seems to be an inescapable part of the human condition.[2] Because of its ability to make new wholes out of contrasting elements, music is the art which most aptly symbolises this quest.

Here, then, is the second of those two important features: the elements of artistic ideas made to work together, combined and contrasted to become the structural forces which sustain the form; and, as we've seen, it is the form which signifies. Incidentally, this may also explain our perception of 'beauty' in nature: disparate elements mysteriously operating together to create something which is more than the sum of the parts. As a medieval translation from the words of the Roman Emperor Marcus Aurelius Antoninus, has it:

> How all things upon Earth are pesle mesle and how miraculously things contrary one to another concurre to the beautie and perfection of this universe.

Thus, we perceive nature functioning like a work of art.

And art is artifice: it is artificial; it is not natural. Unlike science, art does not attempt to explain the natural world but rather to go beyond it, borrowing its shapes, colours, sounds and textures as the raw materials for restless experimentation in the quest for a glimpse of universal form. Art objects are significant not because they show us nature as it might be but because they open windows upon a wholly different level of experience. For that reason, it is the product, not the effort to produce it, that matters.

Stimulating adventurousness of that order, in thinking and making, engaging with great things, and discovering 'harmonies between our

---

2 Anthony Storr, 'Music in Relation to the Self', in *Music and the Cycle of Life: Conference Papers* (London: British Society for Music Therapy, 1988), p. 13.

inner states and our surroundings'[3] has been at the root of our efforts, over the past three decades, to revivify the school music curriculum. Today, the most successful examples of music education are not those in which teachers play for safety with a so-called 'balanced curriculum' but where students are encouraged to take risks; to reach for – as someone said of poetry – 'a sense of possibility beyond the words'.

It took us thirty years to rescue music in schools from being at best a kind of cultural additive to enhance the performance of the educational machine, and at worst mere entertainment – often justified as a necessary relaxation for students from the 'real' business of learning! In the end what brought music to the centre of the curriculum debate was acceptance of the idea that music as music – not as social history or acoustics or 'theory' – has educational potential for all pupils; and in that cause the protagonists were composers: Peter Maxwell Davies, Murray Schafer, George Self, Brian Dennis, and others.

'Anything predictable is not art', declared the always provocative Hans Keller; and, on the subject of his own teaching at one of the London conservatoires, he spoke of 'curing students of their "A" levels and returning them to music'. Sadly, in the rather grey, examination-oriented culture of the present time, we may be in danger of losing them again. A *fin de siècle* decadence seems to have taken hold, calling to mind Harry Partch's brilliantly simple explanation:

> When things are hopping ... definition: the BIG WORLD, complex in excitement, simple in rules, no analysis. When things are not hopping ... definition: the little world, simple in excitement, complex in rules, utter analysis!

Where has the excitement with music gone? What has happened to imagination?

It is not musical merely to train students to read guidebooks or follow signposts: this way sonata, fugue, baroque, and classical. Whatever significance such information has, it is not a musical significance. Pieces of music can only be understood as individual art objects in their own

---

3 Sigfried Giedion, *Space, Time and Architecture: The Growth of a New Tradition* (Cambridge, MA: Harvard University Press, 1967), p. 430.

terms, not by comparing one with another. It is pointless to complain that we can't understand Stravinsky because he doesn't sound like Mozart. The teacher's task is to help students to discover, in every piece they encounter, features which make that particular world whole: the complementariness of elements, revealing their peculiar potential for the developments and transformations which make the music go on in time to create a satisfying form; satisfying because it manifestly fulfils the ideas from which it sprang. In other words, the reason why the black marble staircase was absolutely essential and the oak one would not have worked!

That is the kind of understanding that matters; and, in music, it is best nurtured through first-hand experience of working with musical ideas – in improvising, composing, performing, and in relating that experience to a range of other music.

We have come a long way with music education in this century, and the achievements have been real. They may now be temporarily obscured; but that is precisely the reason why we should hold on to our ideals. Now, more than ever, we need to keep music in schools musical.

# Music: The Breath of Life

WILFRID MELLERS

As a writer, composer and educator Wilfrid Mellers (1914–2008) was a major influence on several generations. He started the music department at York University in 1964 and – as he explains – its curriculum anticipated the current scene where many forms of popular and world music coexist with the Western tradition. Mellers began with a staff of composers – David Blake, Peter Aston, Bernard Rands, Robert Sherlaw Johnson and John Paynter – and soon added performers and ethnomusicologists since he didn't believe in separating theory and practice. His books included studies of Couperin, American music (*Music in a New Found Land*), popular music heroes such as the Beatles and Bob Dylan, and also Bach, Beethoven, Vaughan Williams, Grainger and Poulenc; there are also several anthologies of his writings. Mellers was a composer, too; his *Yeibichai*, commissioned by the BBC for the 1969 Proms, involved a coloratura soprano, a scat singer, an improvising jazz trio, orchestra and tape.

M Y PROFESSIONAL CAREER PARALLELS Sir Frank Callaway's; and since I am even older than he, I can pay heartfelt tribute to the decisive changes that he, more than anyone, effected in the prospects for music education. There can to my mind be no doubt as to what was the most significant change in attitudes to music education that occurred during our careers, hopefully given committed pushes by both of us. To put it crudely, music education became less a study of historical artefacts arranged in chronological sequence, and more a cultivation of music as ongoing activity. Of course, this was part of a general tendency, rampant during the sixties, towards 'creativity' – a recognition that the arts are not specialised fields of knowledge to be passively confronted, but are activities which anyone alive to some degree can and often does participate in. Children, from an early age, draw, paint, and model what they see both 'out there' and within the inner eye; slightly less immediately, they use the words we speak in normal converse to explore, if not define, their place in the world and although music is a pursuit more circumscribed by skills that have to be 'learned', it is possible to create music by using sound-sources on similarly empirical principles. The widening of horizons made this more readily acceptable; awareness of jazz, folk musics, pop musics, and the musics of non-Western, even so-called primitive, cultures has direct bearing on the musical evolution of children, who are by nature small savages. People in Sir Frank's – and my – entourage saw music as a voyage of discovery; everything sprang from that, and I would like to think that divine fires still glow and glimmer, if they no longer crackle.

For, of course, with the passage of years, reaction against 'creativity' – in all fields, not only music – set in and hardened. And it is true that stimulating the imagination and inventiveness of the young is only a starting-point. *Ad hoc* abilities are basic; but executive skills in performance and knowledge of grammar in composition are essential for creative fulfilment, and vaguely benign intentionality cannot take their place. Even so, we must never forget that the primary impulse to musical creation comes from within, and that no prescriptions of law and rule can be ends in themselves. Lighting the fire of the aural imagination is inseparable from experience of (rather than knowledge about) already-created artefacts. We must start from awareness of what music is, and what it is for. We may not think, as do some 'primitive' peoples, that without music the sun would cease to promote fertility, the moon to control the tides; but we can recognise that music – that may be reduced to aural wallpaper, exerting sales-pressure in supermarkets or soothing frayed nerves in terrorist-infested airports – may also reveal to us, through nerves and blood and bone as well as ears, the qualities that make us human. If we can't approach J. S. Bach's definition of music as 'Harmonious Euphony for the Glory of God and the Instruction of my Neighbour', we can still understand what it might mean.

What is wrong with musical education in this country here and now is that Our Leaders, whether in educational fields or in government at large, haven't a clue as to what Bach meant by his definition, nor even what Sir Frank (and I) were on about in considering the future of education in music. Music education no longer receives support in Britain because authority regards it as a trivial pursuit which has no connection with Market Values (which means non-values) and with the accumulation of money. The situation is heart-rending because ironic, since we are in some ways just beginning to reap the fruits of the state-support that was given to music thirty years ago.

The standard of performance in British universities and musical academies is now remarkably high because we are on the crest of the wave that surged through the sixties. The crests of waves can only fall; and as creative brilliance is replaced by more pedestrian endeavour, so the cry will be for more easily measurable and marketable criteria of excellence. I am pessimistic about the chances of resisting this – except when, listening to young people making music, I'm content to believe in what is happening in the moment, and even to think that such youthful vivacity may conquer the powers of darkness: which are currently dark indeed!

At least one can say that few university music departments fail now to recognise that their academic pursuits need to have audible outlets; while, complementarily, academies of music admit that knowledge of musical and cultural history can make for better performance. The snag is the sheer limitation imposed by time. There is now so much musical history that it is impossible, either temporally or geographically, to 'cover the ground'. This is why it is ever more important to start with creation, since it is through doing that one learns what has been, and might be, or ought to be, done.

But whatever the problems involved, we cannot ignore the pluralism of our global village. Not only is awareness of music no longer confined to two and a half European centuries: we are also 'exposed' to a vast number of different phenomena all described as music. It would be foolhardy to expect every student to have experience of all the brands of music from classical to pop to jazz to folk to show business, let alone the multi-ethnic cultures of non-Western communities. Perhaps the only way to tackle this is to start from awareness of music which for various reasons is currently cultivated and to ask WHY this kind of music momentarily appeals to us. For instance, to think and feel about the immense popularity of composers like Górecki, Pärt and Tavener would encourage us to reflect on the state of the modern world in general: and on the reasons why 'fashionable' composers are cultivating techniques originally evolved during the Middle Ages or in relatively primitive, but faith-dominated, communities. From that we'd be led to speculate on how much or little this means. Our approach to medieval music itself, for instance, would mean something in the light of our own experience; similarly, the music of composers like Lou Harrison and Peter Sculthorpe – who are important figures without the 'fabulous' success of a Górecki – would help us to understand why the apparently remote cultures on which they draw for inspiration seem to be coming to terms with our own societies.

The alarming variety of styles cultivated by modern composers can provide insights out of apparent confusion; all our young should create at least a little, and we should encourage them to think, as well as feel, about why they compose in the ways they favour – whether their idiom be conventionally literate in European tradition, or whether it be affiliated to some type of *avant-garde* theatre, or to folk musics, jazz, pop, or any of the 'ethnic' cultures that are behind such activities. We should start from where we are: from what, as creators in sound, we do, and why we do that rather than something else. Such thought and speculation would lead us into a study of many (perhaps unexpected) areas of the past as well as present. Another crucial question would be whether or no we adopt electrophonic techniques, which are products of our time, and how far we think these have 'superseded' straight acoustical approaches. Electrophonics have, of course, further significance in that they are a gateway into many 'commercial' manifestations of music production: from which many young musicians will probably make their living. Can even the TV jingle – not merely film and television music – have artistic as well as mercantile validity? There are composers who think so; and this is a question we have to confront.

If I were today in the process of founding a new department of music in a university or academy, I'd probably base it on principles broadly the same as those I adopted thirty years back. The course would centre around the music of our own time for the obvious reason that it is our music; and it would embrace awareness of the classics of twentieth-century music (acquired by performing as well as studying them), alongside experience (again acquired mainly by doing) of other types of contemporary music founded in folk, jazz, film, television and electrophonic techniques. It wouldn't matter that all these musics might not be equally 'authentic', and that some would prove illusory; all could prove 'educational', in that they help us to understand what we are and where we may be going.

Members of staff who were trained in oral techniques, whether as jazz-men or as ethnomusicologists, would be essential to this undertaking; but so would 'straight' historians and analysts, who would conduct the central classes on Bach, Mozart, Beethoven and the other European figureheads; and so would specialists in Medieval, Renaissance and Baroque musics who could promote 'authentic' approaches to style and performance, not merely as a technical exercise, but with reference to what the people who invented the music thought they were doing with and through it. Comparison between aims and intentions, as displayed by musicians working in so many different fields over so vast a period of time, could never be adequate; but it would at least induce humility. The *musics* of oral traditions can only be taught by making them; and in the long run that applies to literate music also.

The difficulties of our task are revealed in a two-volume work called *Companion to Contemporary Musical Thought*, edited by John Paynter, Tim Howell, Richard Orton, and Peter Seymour, and published by Routledge in 1992. Apart from writing the prefatorial chapter, I had nothing to do with this compilation; but the editors were all members of the staff of the music department I founded at York, Paynter being an educationalist (is that the dreadful word?), Howell an analyst, Orton in charge of the electronic studio, and Seymour responsible for 'performance studies', especially in the Renaissance and Baroque areas. The volumes raise most, perhaps all, of the questions that musicians and teachers will have to confront over the next decade, stimulating awareness that most of us already have. Being aware is not, however, in itself an answer to our problems, since I suspect that Our Leaders are probably oblivious of, and certainly indifferent to, those problems. Music, with or without its 'problems', does not exist in a vacuum. There is some slight comfort in the thought that, while our 'civilisation' cannot survive in any meaningful sense without music, music is not totally dependent on what, with us, passes for civilisation. If ever there was a time when artists ought to be, in Shelley's words, 'unacknowledged legislators of the world', that time is now. Let us pray: not however to the god of any accredited creed, but to Music, which is the BREATH OF LIFE.

# PART V

# TWO REVIEWS OF *BERNARR RAINBOW ON MUSIC*

These reviews are included in this publication as an indicator of Rainbow's achievements fifteen years after his death. Nicholas Temperley exposes some of his idiosyncrasies, in particular his unswerving support of tonic-sol-fa and his tendency to adjust his findings towards his own inclinations. Marie McCarthy takes a generous view of Rainbow's legacy even when, as Temperley points out, he seemed unwilling to credit American developments. She also provides some background for Rainbow's life and work not otherwise available in this volume.

*Music and Letters* 93.2
(August 2012), pp. 241–3

# The Wrong Title?

NICHOLAS TEMPERLEY

Nicholas Temperley is English by birth and holds a PhD from Cambridge
University. From 1967 to 1996 he was a professor at the University of Illinois.
He has published extensively as a musicologist and has been remarkably
influential in raising the profile of nineteenth-century British music. He
has written two seminal books in the field of religious music: *The Music of
the English Parish Church* (Cambridge: Cambridge University Press, 1979),
and *Studies in English Church Music* (Farnham: Ashgate, 2009). Temperley
created and continues to direct the Hymn Tune Index, an online catalogue
of all tunes published for use with English-language hymns between 1535
and 1820. He is now co-editing the first critical edition of the popular
sixteenth-century Sternhold and Hopkins psalm book.

*Bernarr Rainbow on Music: Memoirs and Selected Writings.* By
Bernarr Rainbow, with introductions by Gordon Cox and Charles
Plummeridge, edited by Peter Dickinson, pp. xiii + 398 (The Boydell
Press, Woodbridge, 2010, £25. ISBN 978-1-84383-592-9.)

BERNARR RAINBOW (1914–98) was an important figure in English
musical life, and it has been well worthwhile assembling this tribute to
his work. It takes an unconventional form: two introductory assessments;
an unfinished autobiographical memoir; a reprint of Rainbow's biography
of John Curwen; and a miscellany of his shorter articles and reviews.
Although the editors are naturally motivated by respect and warm feeling
for their subject, their comments include some critical appraisal as well.

Rainbow was an accomplished choral conductor, organist, teacher,
and administrator, and it could be argued that his greatest influence was
conveyed directly through these activities. His teaching methods, his
choice of music for choirs to sing, and his administrative decisions were
practical expressions of strongly held and often controversial views that he
secms to have formed early in life. At the same time he sought to justify
these ideas in his research and writing, where his gifts were also of a high

order. But objectivity was often a casualty of his partisanship. This was true for both his areas of historical interest: music education and Anglican church music.

His work on music education was first brought forward in 1967, when his master's thesis at the University of Leicester was expanded to form his first book, *The Land without Music: Musical Education in England, 1800–1860*. I could never quite forgive him for using this disgraceful and wholly inappropriate title, which appeared just at a time when I was trying to show, almost single-handedly, that England was not, and never had been, a land without music – a point that I think has by now been abundantly demonstrated. I expressed my indignation in a *Musical Times* review, and I needn't repeat it here.[1] It did not affect my personal fondness for the author, nor my admiration of the book itself, which opened up an entirely unfamiliar aspect of musical history.

Rainbow showed convincingly how the tonic sol-fa system, based on the 'movable doh' principle, where *doh* always represents the keynote, is inherently superior (for teaching singing) to 'fixed doh' systems, where *doh* always represents C. Despite this irrefutable fact, John Hullah's fixed-doh system, following French models, was officially adopted by the government and for long prevailed in the vast majority of English schools. Rainbow identified the pioneer of tonic sol-fa in Sarah Glover, a previously unknown Norwich schoolteacher, and its strongest advocate in John Curwen, a nonconformist minister who disclaimed any technical understanding of music. This intriguing story is retold with many new details and arguments in Rainbow's biography of Curwen, reprinted here, and in some of the shorter publications included in the book. One of the most significant of his later discoveries was that tonic sol-fa was the basis of Zoltán Kodály's educational methods, through which it gained far greater influence than most people had suspected. The historical importance of the system has been reaffirmed and enhanced by Charles McGuire's recent book, *Music and Victorian Philanthropy* (Cambridge, 2009).

Although tonic sol-fa eventually succeeded in England, it never fully replaced traditional music notation in school teaching, as Rainbow thought it should. In his passionate advocacy he forgot that instrumental music

---

1 *Musical Times* 109, no. 1502 (April 1968), 337–8.

can also have an important place in children's education, in classes as well as individual teaching, and that much worthwhile vocal music is modal, modulates frequently, or is even atonal. These facts limit the value of tonic sol-fa. Even if it is more difficult to learn sight-singing from traditional notation, students who overcome the difficulties have a clear advantage for further musical development over those who only know tonic sol-fa. But Rainbow was not willing to give such arguments serious consideration. He remained certain that the voice and the 'inner ear' were the only true foundations of musicality (which perhaps they are), and that a teaching method that facilitated their cultivation in early youth was the only one that should be used (a more debatable point). This position is illustrated in the subtitle of his book: though it claims to cover 'Musical Education in England' – a potentially wide-ranging topic – the book is in fact entirely restricted to the teaching of sight-singing.

Rainbow openly gloried in tonic sol-fa as a uniquely English achievement. So it was. But Gordon Cox, in his introduction to the selection of Rainbow's articles, rightly praises 'his ability to work across national boundaries' (p. 141), citing the many Continental works discussed in Rainbow's 1989 book, *Music in Educational Thought and Practice* (new, enlarged edition with Gordon Cox, 2006) and included in his series of forty-five *Classic Texts in Music Education*. There is, however, a curious exception. In both the book and the series Rainbow consistently ignored American developments in the field, which have been at least as remarkable as those in Britain and have included a long series of pioneering educational practices. In particular, shape-note notation, using distinctively shaped note-heads on the staff to represent *mi, fa, sol, la*, anticipated Sarah Glover in the use of a movable-doh system by more than two decades, starting with William Little and William Smith's *The Easy Instructor, or A New Method of Teaching Sacred Harmony* (Philadelphia, 1801). It was wildly successful in teaching under-educated rural Americans to sing simple songs in harmony, and it has outlived the effective demise of tonic sol-fa notation, being still widely used by Sacred Harp singers. It has the additional advantage of simultaneously teaching its practitioners the fundamentals of staff notation. But I have found no mention of shape-notes in any of Rainbow's works. His principle of giving credit where credit is due did not, it seems, extend to Americans.

In his other major field, Rainbow again published a pioneering work, *The Choral Revival in the Anglican Church, 1839–72* (1970), and followed it up with shorter offerings. The book uncovered much new material about the musical ideals and practices of the Tractarian movement. As Charles Plummeridge points out (p. 6), 'To some extent he devised his own research methods and tracked down materials in markets and second-hand book-shops.' Though this shows admirable independence and determination, it also suggests a reason for the book's undoubted bias towards the party to which Rainbow himself was attached. In his searches among the vast surviving data of the period, he mainly looked for what appealed to him. As director of music at the College of St Mark and St John, Chelsea, he had discovered a diary of service music written by his predecessor, Thomas Helmore. The work of Helmore, his brother, and their fellow Tractarians such as Frederick Oakeley, W. J. E. Bennett, William Dyce, and J. M. Neale soon became his main preoccupation in research. He reached the surprising conclusion that 'The choral revival of the nineteenth century may hence be seen as directly connected with two other contemporary events: the Oxford Movement, which gave rise to it; and the acceptance of state responsibility for national education, which made its realisation possible' (*Choral Revival*, p. 6). It is no coincidence that these two factors represented Rainbow's principal fields of historical (and professional) interest.

But as far as the great majority of churches were concerned, 'the choral revival of the nineteenth century' consisted in the main of increasingly grand and elaborate music performed by choir and organ, including anthems, canticle settings, responses, and psalms sung to harmonized Anglican chants, all in imitation of the established traditions of cathedral music. The congregation, as before, would sing chiefly in the hymns, but with slowly growing skill. This was far removed from the Tractarian goal of congregational singing of all the liturgy to austere, unaccompanied Gregorian chants. Such an ideal could be achieved by the specialised congregation at St Mark's, and at a few churches and chapels populated by dedicated and well-educated Tractarians, but it could never become the norm for the whole Church. Apart from the technical difficulties of chanting prose for unskilled singers, the idiom was simply too remote from what people knew and loved. 'The emptiness of that incautious claim was quickly acknowledged', as Rainbow has said of another attempt at improvement (p. 361).

The Victorian triumph of choral church music, then, was in no sense a product of the Oxford Movement, which, indeed, often opposed it. It was partly due to traditional (non-Tractarian) high churchmen like John Jebb and Walter Hook, as Rainbow recognised in his book and in a later article reprinted here ('John Jebb and the Choral Service'). What Rainbow altogether failed or refused to see was that other parties and historical trends contributed a great deal to the ultimate result. As early as 1716 the prominent clergyman Thomas Bisse had urged that 'parish churches should, as much as possible, conform to the customs of the cathedral churches', and this ideal would guide many attempts at improvement in the following century and a half. Voluntary choirs were assembled; organs were purchased, replaced by bands or barrel organs in less affluent parishes; anthems were widely introduced; congregational chanting of psalms was initiated by Evangelicals in the north of England. The general increase in material prosperity raised aesthetic standards. Upwardly mobile Victorian families wished to see their improved situation reflected in their parish churches as much as in the rest of their lives; musical conventions were imported from the theatre and concert hall, and from abroad. Romantic antiquarians, long before the Oxford Movement, began to revive early music.

All this was pointed out, with abundant documentation, in my book, *The Music of the English Parish Church* (Cambridge, 1979), but Rainbow characteristically ignored these findings. His 1995 article 'In Quires and Places Where They Sing: Some Historical Aspects of Anglican Church Music' is presented as an objective historical survey. In fact it is a promotional essay, in which every attempt to improve Anglican church music (other than that of the early Victorian Anglo-Catholics) is either passed over or shown in the worst possible light, by selective reading of primary sources, unflattering quotations from hostile or facetious writers, crudely pejorative phrases such as 'cock-and-hen choirs', 'a gimcrack anthem', 'pocket Romanticism' (pp. 361, 363, 380), and much more of the same kind, the whole illustrated by two or three caricature engravings. Incidentally, there are factual errors as well – Merbecke's *Book of Common Praier Noted* was not designed for congregational singing (pp. 356–7). This article is an extreme case, but it should serve as a warning that Rainbow's writings cannot always be relied on for fairness or historical truth.

For me the most enjoyable part of this book, by far, is *Salute to Life*, the memoir that Rainbow began to write shortly before he died, at the urging of his former colleague Peter Dickinson. It is charming, humorous, modest, mercifully free of polemics, and gives a vivid picture of Rainbow's youth and middle age (it ends in 1972). His experiences in the army during the Second World War, which Plummeridge says he rarely talked about; his vacillations regarding his career; his post-war work as organist and music master in High Wycombe: all tell us much that is fresh about their time and place, as well as explaining something of the author's complex character. This eighty-three-page autobiography is a real page-turner.

## ■ Addendum by Nicholas Temperley

In June 1965 the *Musical Times* published a letter from Bernarr Rainbow asking about the origin of the phrase 'das Land ohne Musik' in reference to England.[2] Charles Cudworth in reply cited a book with that title by Oscar A. H. Schmitz, published in Munich in 1914. Of course, the idea behind the phrase was widely held for a long time before that, both in Britain and on the Continent. Among other writers, including Percy Young, I have surveyed the history of the notion and speculated as to its origin.[3]

Schmitz (1873–1931) was a historian and essayist, not a musicologist, still less a musician. His book is not about music. It is a largely admiring analysis of English culture, society, and politics. He praises many English qualities such as tolerance, lack of envy, and progressive spirit, which he contrasts with the German character. In one of the few references to music he says: 'Nowhere ... is music more highly esteemed than in England. The least skill in piano-playing or singing at times suffices to make of someone the lion of a "week-end" party in the country. With what persistence you

---

2 *Musical Times* 106, no. 1468 (June 1965), 446. Most writers of that time said 'England' when they meant 'Britain', as some still do; I am here following this custom only when referring to another writer's opinion or statement.

3 Percy M. Young, *A History of British Music* (London: Ernest Benn, 1967), p. 281; N. Temperley, 'Xenophilia in British Musical History', in *Nineteenth-Century British Music Studies*, vol. 1, ed. Bennett Zon (Aldershot: Ashgate, 1999), pp. 1–19.

sometimes hear a young lady practising, but soon you find her out; so much zeal, combined with so little talent, can only be explained on the assumption that she is totally unmusical; otherwise she could not bear her own strumming.'⁴ This was probably based on Schmitz's experiences in 1910, the only time he had visited Britain. He seems to have been unaware of the extraordinary advances in British music and musical life of the past few decades. But then he did not pretend to have carried out a wide-ranging study of contemporary British musical culture.

The motive for Rainbow's query became apparent in 1967, when his book *The Land without Music* appeared. The idea that the English were congenitally unmusical still prevailed in some quarters. Even in academic circles it was widely believed that there was a 'Dark Age of English Music' between Handel and Elgar, chiefly because the period had produced no British composers of lasting and unquestioned stature. That in itself is not, of course, a reliable measure of a country's musical vitality. Nevertheless, I for one had long refused to accept that all the music composed in Britain over a period of more than a century was worthless. I had devoted some of my energies to rediscovering and reviving forgotten composers such as George Frederick Pinto, Henry Hugo Pierson and Edward James Loder, and re-evaluating the work of John Field, the Wesleys, Sterndale Bennett, and many others. Not surprisingly, I was quite angered by Rainbow's choice of such a title just when I was in the midst of mounting an attack on the point of view it expressed. After more than fifty years I have come to realize that it is almost a hopeless task to try to overcome such a deep-seated prejudice. The classical canon is so entrenched that only a small minority of music lovers can be induced to give a fair hearing to unfamiliar music by contemporaries of the great composers. But in my youth I was still hoping to effect a full revival of Victorian musical products, and here was a book that, judging by its title, was reinforcing the misguided and reactionary opposition.

The real proof that Britain has never been a land without music has come from the explosion of research over the last thirty years into British performance history, institutions, journalism, domestic life, education,

---

4 Oscar A. H. Schmitz, *The Land without Music*, trans. H. Herzl (London: Jarrolds, 1925), pp. 17–18.

and many other areas. It has shown conclusively that music played a large and important part in the life of the Georgians and the Victorians, and was highly valued by them – a point that even Schmitz had to concede in the passage quoted above.

Who were the pioneers and models in this rediscovery of Victorian musical life? One of them was none other than our friend Bernarr Rainbow, who offered penetrating new studies of music education and Anglican choral music based on documentary evidence. In each case he showed how important music was in an aspect of British life in the nineteenth century. He was on our side; he was one of us. It remains a complete mystery why he chose as a title for his first book a phrase that seemed to deny the significance of its own contents, and to fortify the very prejudice that he was helping to question. This was indeed *Der Titel ohne Bedeutung*.[5]

5 The title without significance.

*Journal of Historical Research in Music Education*
33.1 (October 2011), pp. 89–92.

# An American Perspective

## MARIE MCCARTHY

> Marie McCarthy is Professor of Music Education at the University of Michigan, where she teaches courses on general music, research design, and music cultures in the classroom. Her research studies address the historical, social, and cultural foundations of music education, the transmission of music in cultural context, and spiritual dimensions of music education. Her publications include two books, *Passing It On: The Transmission of Music in Irish Culture* (Cork: Cork University Press, 2009), and *Toward a Global Community: A History of the International Society for Music Education, 1953–2003* (ISME, 2003).

*Bernarr Rainbow on Music: Memoirs and Selected Writings.* Ed. Peter Dickinson. Introductions by Gordon Cox and Charles Plummeridge. Woodbridge, UK; Rochester, NY: Boydell Press, 2010. xiii + 398 pp. Index, hardback. ISBN 978-1-84383-592-9, $45.00.

B ERNARR RAINBOW (1914–98) was a leading historian of music education in the twentieth century. As Allen P. Britton (1914–2003) established the field of music education history in the United States, Rainbow spent much of his career following a similar path in Britain during the same time period. His enormous output of authored and edited books and other writings is celebrated in *Bernarr Rainbow on Music: Memoirs and Selected Writings.* This is the third book devoted to Rainbow's writings published by Boydell Press under the aegis of the Bernarr Rainbow Trust and the editorship of Peter Dickinson. Together with the other two books, *Music in Educational Thought and Practice*: Bernarr Rainbow with Gordon Cox (2006) and *Four Centuries of Music Teaching Manuals, 1518–1932* (2009), they represent a major contribution to the field and a valuable addition to primary source literature in music education.

In the foreword to this volume, the general editor Peter Dickinson provides a context for the publication, especially the writing of the memoir, and lists sources for the contents of the book. Organized in three parts, part 1 is introduced by Charles Plummeridge and includes Rainbow's memoir, *A Salute to Life*, written shortly before his death in 1998. Part 2 is a reprint of his 1980 monograph, *John Curwen: A Short Critical Biography*, an appropriate choice for a scholar who dedicated much of his scholarly work to Curwen's contributions to music pedagogy. In his introduction to part 3, *Selected Writings*, Gordon Cox states that when he chose Rainbow's writings, he focused chiefly on his 'two principal fields, the history of music education and the history of Anglican church music' (p. 140).

In his introduction to Rainbow's personal memoir in part 1, Plummeridge summarises the significance of Rainbow's contributions as teacher, researcher, and teacher educator. He provides a biographical sketch of Rainbow, which serves as an excellent prelude to the memoir. This is especially true for readers not familiar with the details of his life or with the development of British music education history during the twentieth century. By making reference to Rainbow's books and other publications, Plummeridge exposes the magnitude of his life's work. The memoir, *A Salute to Life: Sketches Toward a Personal Memoir*, is divided into nine chapters that describe Rainbow's life up to 1972. In that year, he left his post at the College of St Mark and St John where he had been director of music since 1952. Dickinson encouraged him to write the memoir and explains that Rainbow felt unable to continue the memoir after 1972 (p. ix). Dickinson also explains that he added the footnotes to clarify references in the text, with the exception of those footnotes initialled BR. The footnotes are of immense value to the reader as a reminder of Rainbow's publications and as background for related events and developments in his life.

The nine chapters are arranged according to the various stages of Rainbow's life from 1914 to 1972. The first two record memories of his childhood and school years. In these and other chapters, Rainbow's ability to remember the events and happenings of his life in great detail is extraordinary. As he describes his own life, he also situates it in the context of education and culture at the time. This is most valuable and adds depth and interest to the memoir. After a short time working in the Land Registry, Rainbow was called up and joined the army in 1939. Chapters 3 through 5 are devoted to his life in the army and his travels between 1939 and 1944 when he was discharged and returned to Britain. His years at High Wycombe as organist and choirmaster of All Saints Parish Church and head of music at the Royal Grammar School, 1944–52, are documented in chapter 6. In chapters 7 through 9, Rainbow writes a lively narrative describing his career as the director of music at the College of St Mark and St John, Chelsea, the Church of England College of Education connected to the Institute of Education, University of London. Rainbow ends his memoir with a reference to an invitation he received to write, 'some forty articles, biographical notices, and factual entries' (p. 91) for the new edition of Grove's dictionary. Such an invitation was testimony to his international scholarly reputation and his vast knowledge of British music history and culture.

Rainbow's critical biography of John Curwen forms part 2 of the book. The original book was published in 1980, the centenary year of Curwen's death. He was a strong advocate of Curwen and what he stood for in music pedagogy. Rainbow wanted 'to press for the restoration of his work to its neglected place in the music curriculum' (p. 134). In this work, Rainbow was a revisionist in that he took the *Memorials of John Curwen*, authored by Curwen's son, John Spencer Curwen, and 'widened the range of enquiry' to gain a more objective account. The critical nature of the revision is evident in the thematic approach he applies to the biography, with topics such as challenge, action, struggle, and achievement, each matched with a time period in his life. The appendix to the biography, 'A Visit to Miss Glover's School', published originally in 1842, is a gem. The reader gets a firsthand view of Sarah Glover teaching in her classroom, a rare kind of primary source available to us from the nineteenth century.

In part 3 of the book, Gordon Cox chose writings from Rainbow's œuvre related to music in schools and churches, 'the most substantial part of his output' (p. 140), and a small number about musical life in London. He arranged them according to themes rather than chronology: Reflections on Historical Research in Music Education, School Music Abroad, Music Education in Nineteenth-Century England, Music Education in Twentieth-Century Britain, Music Teaching Methods, Nineteenth-Century Musical Life in London, and Church Music. Cox addresses each of the themes in his introduction (pp. 140–6) and explains how each constituted a foundation for Rainbow's output and how he grouped articles together under the same theme. For example, in the section titled School Music Abroad, Cox says he grouped articles 'which I consider to be one of Rainbow's main strengths, his ability to work across national boundaries with an impressive range of sources' (p. 141). In another section, Music Education in Nineteenth-Century England, Cox considers Rainbow to be 'on his favourite ground' (p. 141). Cox also points out that Rainbow was an activist and wanted to influence curricular practice, 'albeit in a somewhat conservative and traditionalist fashion' (p. 146). In a similar vein, Dickinson and Plummeridge describe Rainbow's criticisms of music education practices and, in turn, those who criticised his traditional attitude to musical values. Plummeridge writes: 'He was well aware of such observations and in the memoir he takes a mischievous delight in supporting elitist positions' (p. 5).

Cox prepares the reader for the ideas they will encounter in Rainbow's articles when he writes: 'Some will agree with his interpretations, others will disagree. But hopefully what will shine through is the sheer commitment, energy and integrity Rainbow brought to his task as a researcher and practitioner' (p. 146). The magnitude of this scholar's work is humbling, his writings are testimony to his passion for music teaching and scholarship, and his advocacy for high standards in music education thought and practice was a constant theme throughout his life.

To bring this great scholar to life for the reader, editor Peter Dickinson includes a series of nineteen plates (as well as a frontispiece), which are inserted between pages 50 and 51. They are arranged chronologically and provide images that illuminate Rainbow's early childhood, his time in the army, his family, his career in music teaching, and receiving the DLitt from the University of Leicester. The jacket illustrations provide a rich context for the contents of the book – Bernarr Rainbow and his life in music, teaching, and scholarship.

The volume celebrates and honours the life and contributions of Bernarr Rainbow in a manner that reflects his unique and honoured place in the history of music and music education in Britain, and in the world of music education history at large. By the magnificent structure and aesthetic appearance of the book, as well as the care that was taken to contextualize Rainbow's writings, the general editor, Peter Dickinson, and Charles Plummeridge and Gordon Cox have produced an important work, one that deserves close examination and wide recognition by scholars of music education.

# APPENDICES

# Classic Texts in Music Education

Edited with introductions by Bernarr Rainbow
Series Editor: Peter Dickinson

1  Jean-Jacques Rousseau, *Project Concerning New Symbols for Music* (1742) (*Projet concernant de nouveaux signes pour la musique*), trans. Bernarr Rainbow

2  Bernarr Rainbow and various authors: *English Psalmody Prefaces: Popular Methods of Teaching, 1562–1835*

3  William Bathe, *A Briefe Introduction to the Skill of Song* (c. 1587), ed. Bernarr Rainbow

4  Loys Bourgeois, *The Direct Road to Music* (1550) (*Le droict chemin de musique*), trans. Bernarr Rainbow

5  Sarah Glover, *Scheme for Rendering Psalmody Congregational* (1835) together with *The Sol-fa Tune Book* (1839)

6  John Turner, *A Manual of Instruction in Vocal Music* (1833)

7  John Hullah, *Wilhem's Method of Teaching Singing* (1842)

8  Pierre Galin, *Rationale for a New Way of Teaching Music* (1818) (from *Exposition d'une nouvelle méthode pour l'ensignement de la musique*), trans. Bernarr Rainbow

9  Joseph Mainzer, *Singing for the Million* (1841)

10  W. E. Hickson, *The Singing Master* (1836)

11  M. A. Langdale and S. Macpherson, *Early Essays on Musical Appreciation* (1908–15)

12  Joseph Mainzer, *Music and Education* (1848)

13  F.-J. Fétis, *Music explained to the World* (1844) (*La musique mise à la portée de tout le monde*)

14  John Curwen, *Singing for Schools and Congregations: a Grammar of Vocal Music with a Course of Lessons and Exercises* (1843, edition of 1852)

15  John Spenser Curwen and John Hullah, *School Music Abroad* (1879–1901)

16  William Crotch, *Substance of Several Courses of Lectures on Music* (1831)

17  David Baptie, *A Handbook of Musical Biography* (1883)

18  William Cooke Stafford, *A History of Music* (1830)
19  John Curwen, *The Teacher's Manual of the Tonic Sol-fa Method: Dealing with the Art of Teaching and the Teaching of Music* (1875)
20  Bernarr Rainbow and various authors, *Music and the English Public School* (1990) [New, enlarged edition in progress]
21  Martin Agricola, *The Rudiments of Music* (1539) (*Rudimenta musices*), trans. John Trowell
22  *Four Centuries of Music Teaching Manuals, 1518–1932*, ed. Bernarr Rainbow, with an introduction by Gordon Cox. Boydell, 2009
23  Bernarr Rainbow with Gordon Cox, *Music in Educational Thought and Practice: a Survey from 800 BC*, 2nd enlarged edition, foreword by Sir Peter Maxwell Davies. Boydell, 2006; paperback, 2007
24  *Music Education in Crisis: the Bernarr Rainbow Lectures and Other Assessments*, ed. Peter Dickinson. Boydell, 2013
25  William Crotch, *Elements of Musical Composition* (2nd edition, 1830)
26  *Sir Arthur Somervell on Music Education: his Writings, Speeches and Letters*, foreword by Elizabeth Jane Howard, ed. Gordon Cox, Boydell, 2003
27  *Bernarr Rainbow on Music: Memoirs and Selected Writings*, ed. Peter Dickinson, with introductions by Gordon Cox and Charles Plummeridge, Boydell, 2010

The above titles are available separately from Boydell & Brewer. Some renumbering has been necessary: orders should include titles.

☐ ☐☐☐☐☐☐☐☐☐☐☐☐☐☐☐☐☐☐☐☐☐☐☐☐☐☐☐☐☐☐☐☐☐☐☐☐☐☐☐☐☐☐

Rainbow's introductions to what he envisaged as the complete series of forty-five texts are collected in *Four Centuries of Teaching Manuals, 1518–1932*, with an introduction by Gordon Cox (Boydell, 2009). Since Rainbow selected his texts, some of these have been published or made available online: more are likely to follow in the Rainbow series or elsewhere. These details are included below with the full series.

1518   Georg Rhau, *Enchiridion utrisque musica practicae* [Can be downloaded in Latin]
1539   Martin Agricola, *The Rudiments of Music (Rudimenta musices)* [CTME 21]

| 1550 | Loys Bourgeois, *The Direct Road to Music (Le droict chemin de musique)* [CTME 4] |
| 1562–1835 | Bernarr Rainbow and various authors, *English Psalmody Prefaces: Popular Methods of Teaching, 1562-1835* [CTME 2] |
| 1587 | William Bathe, *A Briefe Introduction to the Skill of Song* [CTME 3] |
| 1731 | J. C. Pepusch, *A Treatise on Harmony* [published: Gale Ecco, 2010] |
| 1742 | Jean-Jacques Rousseau, *Project Concerning New Symbols for Music (Projet concernant de nouveaux signes pour la musique)* [CTME 1] |
| 1803 | Anne Gunn, *Introduction to Music* [published: Rarebooksclub. com, 2010] |
| 1806 | A. F. C. Kollmann, *A New Theory of Musical Harmony* [microfilm: Library of Congress, 1979] |
| 1806 | J. W. Callcott, *A Musical Grammar in Four Parts* |
| 1809 | H. G. Nägeli, (i) *Die Pestalozzische Gesangbildungslehre* |
| 1810 | H. G. Nägeli, (ii) *Gesangbildungslehre* |
| 1812 | William Crotch, *Elements of Musical Composition* [CTME 25] |
| 1815 | J. B. Logier, *Companion to the Patent Royal Chiroplast* [Euing Collection, University of Glasgow] |
| 1818 | Pierre Galin, *Rationale for a New Way of Teaching Music* (from *Exposition d'une nouvelle méthode*) [CTME 8] |
| 1819 | J. Kemp, *The New System of Musical Education* [published: Kessinger, 2009] |
| 1819 | M. P. (Dorothy Kilner), *The Child's Introduction to Thorough Bass* |
| 1824 | Edouard Jue de Berneval, *La musique apprise sans maître* |
| 1830 | F.-J. Fétis, *Music explained to the World (La musique mise à la portée de tout le monde)* [CTME 13] |
| 1830 | William Cooke Stafford, *A History of Music* [CTME 18] |
| 1831 | William Crotch, *Substance of Several Courses of Lectures on Music* [CTME 16] |
| 1833 | John Turner, *A Manual of Instruction in Vocal Music* [CTME 6] |
| 1835/39 | Sarah Glover, *Scheme for Rendering Psalmody Congregational* together with *The Sol-fa Tune Book* [CTME 5] |

1836    W. E. Hickson, *The Singing Master* [CTME 10]

1836    A. Rodwell, *The Juvenile Pianist*

1839    Adolph Bernhard Marx, *The Universal School of Music* (*Allgemeine Musiklehre*, trans. 1853) [published: Kessinger, 2010; Lightning Source, 2012 etc.]

1841    Joseph Mainzer, *Singing for the Million* [CTME 9]

1842    John Hullah, *Wilhem's Method of Teaching Singing* [CTME 7]

1843    John Curwen, *Singing for Schools and Congregations: a Grammar of Vocal Music with a Course of Lessons and Exercises* [CTME 14]

1844    Mme E. Chevé, *Méthode élémentaire de musique vocale* [online in French: Nabu Press, 2012]

1846    Alfred Day, *Treatise on Harmony* [Cambridge University Press, 2012]

1846    James Turle and Edward Taylor, *The Singing Book*

1848    Joseph Mainzer, *Music and Education* [CTME 12]

1853    Moritz Hauptmann, *The Nature of Harmony and Metre* (*Die Natur der Harmonik und der Metrik*, trans. 1888) [published: Nabu Press, 2010]

1855    Anon (Sarah Mary Fitton), *Conversations on Harmony*

1875    John Curwen, *The Teacher's Manual of the Tonic Sol-fa Method: Dealing with the Art of Teaching and the Teaching of Music* [CTME 19]

1876    E. L. Shedlock, *A Trip to Music Land* [Internet Archive, Cornell University Library, 2008]

1879–1901 John Spencer Curwen and John Hullah, *School Music Abroad* [CTME 15]

1882    Mrs Frederick Inman, *Plan for Teaching Music to a Child*

1883    David Baptie, *A Handbook of Musical Biography* [CTME 17]

1888–1952 Bernarr Rainbow and various authors, *Music and the English Public School* [CTME 20] New, enlarged edition in progress, as *Music in the Independent School: a Celebration,* ed. Andrew Morris.

1903    Hermann Kretzschmar, *Musikalische Zeitfragen* [in German, Nabu, 2010; Kessinger, 2011; General Books LLC, 2012]

1908–15 M. A. Langdale and S. Macpherson, *Early Essays on Musical Appreciation* [CTME 11]

1927    J. H. Borland, *Musical Foundations*
1932    A. Somervell, *Sir Arthur Somervell on Music Education: his*
*Writings, Speeches, and Letters*, foreword by Elizabeth Jane
Howard, ed. Gordon Cox [CTME 26]

## ■ Books by Bernarr Rainbow

*Music in the Classroom*. Heinemann, 1956, r/1960, 1966, 1968, 2nd
edition 1971
*The Land without Music: Musical Education in England, 1800–60, and its*
*Continental Antecedents*. Novello, 1967, r/Boethius, 1991/Boydell, 1997
*The Choral Revival in the Anglican Church, 1839–72*. Oxford University
Press, 1970; r/Boydell, 2001
*John Curwen: a Short Critical Biography*. Novello, 1980, r/Boydell, 2010
[in *Bernarr Rainbow on Music: Memoirs and Selected Writings*]
*Music in Educational Thought and Practice: a Survey from 800 BC*, 2nd
enlarged edition with Gordon Cox; foreword by Sir Peter Maxwell
Davies. Boydell, 2006; paperback, 2007
*Four Centuries of Music Teaching Manuals, 1518–1932*, with an introduction
by Gordon Cox (Boydell, 2009)
*Bernarr Rainbow on Music: Memoirs and Selected Writings*, ed. Peter
Dickinson, with introductions by Gordon Cox and Charles
Plummeridge. Boydell, 2010

## ■ Archives

The Bernarr Rainbow Archive is at the Library of the Institute of Education,
University of London; his family papers are at Hampton Court; and his
collection of Christian and Jewish Hymnals and other Liturgical Music is
at the Maughan Library, King's College, London.

# Awards Made by The Bernarr Rainbow Trust, 1997–2012

- Grants towards the publication of books
  (now all Boydell Press, general editor Peter Dickinson)

2001   Reprint of Bernarr Rainbow, *The Choral Revival in the Anglican Church*

2003   *Sir Arthur Somervell on Music Education* – preface by Rainbow, plus material by Gordon Cox, foreword by Elizabeth Jane Howard

2006   Bernarr Rainbow, *Music in Educational Thought and Practice* – enlarged edition with new material from Gordon Cox, foreword by Sir Peter Maxwell Davies, introduction by Peter Dickinson

2007   Reprint of *A Briefe Introduction to the Skill of Song* (c. 1587), foreword by Rainbow

2007   Paperback of Rainbow, *Music in Educational Thought and Practice*

2009   Bernarr Rainbow, *Four Centuries of Music Teaching Manuals, 1518–1932* – introduction by Gordon Cox

2010   Bernarr Rainbow, *Bernarr Rainbow on Music: Memoirs and Selected Writings, with Introductions by Gordon Cox and Charles Plummeridge* – edited by Peter Dickinson

2013   Peter Dickinson (ed.), *Music Education in Crisis*

2013   Andrew Morris (ed.), *Music in the Independent School: A Celebration* – enlarged edition of *Music in the English Public School*, ed. Bernarr Rainbow (in preparation)

■ Grants to established bodies for specific education projects

1998 Aldeburgh Festival Anniversary Appeal – education facilities at Snape Maltings

1999 Research in Musical Improvisation: Issues and Methodologies – one-day conference, University of Reading

2000 Aldeburgh Productions Education 1, with Glyndebourne – Benjamin Britten, *Peter Grimes* (four-year A-level project)

2001 Aldeburgh Productions Education 2 – Benjamin Britten, *Rape of Lucretia* (A-level project)

2001 British Federation of Youth Choirs – training towards Schools Prom, Royal Albert Hall

2001 Community Opera Project, Gravesend

2002 Aldeburgh Productions Education 3 – festival repertoire project

2002 King's College for the Arts and Technology, Guildford – 'Body and Soul' project

2003 Aldeburgh Productions Education 4 – Henry Purcell, *Gloriana* (A-level project)

2004 Aldeburgh Productions Education 5 – grant towards *Let's Make an Opera*

2004 Institute of Education Library – to create a catalogue of the Rainbow Archive: *Papers of Bernarr Rainbow (1914–1998)*, compiled by Jude Brimmer

2004 Trinity College of Music, Greenwich – for the opening event, with music, of the Bernarr Rainbow Room, endowed with pictures and his memorabilia

2005 Jubilee Opera, Suffolk, 1 – Malcolm Williamson, *The Happy Prince*

2005 Organ Appeal at St James', Muswell Hill – for education work with local schools by Jennifer Bate

2006 Aldeburgh Productions Education, A Celebration of Schools Music – string quartet tuition

2006 Jubilee Opera, Suffolk 2 – Sir Richard Rodney Bennett, *All the King's Men*; Jonathan Wilcocks, *The Pied Piper*

2006 The Holst Birthplace Museum, Cheltenham – for its Schools Music Education programme

2006 The National Youth Orchestra 1 – tuition in workshops, sectionals & ensemble

2006 The Park Lane Group 1 – Young Artists programmes, Purcell Room, London

2006 The Temple Church, London 1 – three-year project training boy choristers

2007 Jubilee Opera, Suffolk, 3

2007 Northumbrian Ranters (traditional music group run by Northumberland County Council)

2007 St Giles, Cripplegate – organ fund and education projects

2007 The Bryceson Organ Appeal – to rescue an 1860s instrument and place it in St Dominic's Prior, London, where it is used for educational purposes

2007 The National Youth Orchestra 2 – tuition in workshops, sectionals & ensemble

2007 The Park Lane Group 2 – Young Artists programmes

2007 The Temple Church, London 2

2008 Aldeburgh Music – project for young musicians in A Celebration of Schools Music

2008 Jubilee Opera 4 – fiftieth-anniversary production of Benjamin Britten, *Noye's Fludde*

2008 The National Youth Orchestra 3

2008 The Temple Church, London 3

2009 Aldeburgh Music – project for young musicians in A Celebration of Schools Music

2009 Aldeburgh Music – tuition for young performers

2009 Britten–Pears Chamber Choir – primary-school children participating

2009 CBSO Youth Orchestra – concert in memory of Dr Nigel Fortune

2009 Dartington Hall Trust 1 – for student bursaries

2009 London String Quartet Foundation 1 – for young players

2009  National Concert of Brass Band Festival

2009  National Youth Choirs – for students

2009  Park Lane Group 3 – Young Artists January series

2009  Royal Opera House Foundation 1 – for youth project

2010  Aberystwyth Music Festival 1 – bursaries for students

2010  Amber Trust (for blind children)

2010  Dartington Hall Trust 2 – student bursaries

2010  Hackney Proms concert series

2010  Keele Concerts Society – programme for percussion in Staffordshire schools

2010  National Youth Choirs

2010  Organ Restoration Fund – for an eighteenth-century instrument in Devon

2010  Park Lane Group Young Artists 4 – Samuel Barber centenary concert, Wigmore Hall

2010  Reading Minster Choral Foundation 1 – for establishing an all-male choir

2010  Royal Opera House Foundation 2 – youth project

2010  Royal Tunbridge Symphony Orchestra – commissioned work for young performers

2010  Verdehr Trio – master-classes at Trinity Laban College

2011  Aldeburgh Music – young musicians course

2011  Friends of St James', Muswell Hill – organ education project

2011  Hallé Concerts Society – 'Come & Play' project

2011  International Organ Festival, St Albans – education programme

2011  Jubilee Opera – for Suffolk children

2011  Keele University schools programme

2011  Lichfield Festival for Young Artists

2011  London String Quartet Foundation 2

2011  Park Lane Group – Young Artists January series

2011  Reading Minster Choral Foundation 2 – lessons for choristers

2011  Wilton's Music Hall Trust – music education programme

2012 Aberystwith Music Festival 2 – student bursaries
2012 Aldeburgh Young Musicians – chamber music
2012 Armonico Consort – running and founding choirs in schools
2012 CBSO Youth Choir
2012 Elgar Birthplace Museum 1 – schools programmes
2012 Hallé Concerts Society – youth-choir training
2012 Holst Birthplace Trust 1 – schools programmes
2012 John Ireland Trust – promoting young performers
2012 Jubilee Opera – opera with primary-school children in Suffolk
2012 London Bach Choir – student bursaries
2012 London String Quartet Foundation 3
2012 Mahogany Opera – children's choir in Britten's *Church Parables*
2012 Oxford Lieder Festival – for young artists
2012 Reading Minster Choral Foundation 3 – lessons for choristers
2012 Royal Opera House Foundation 3 – for young performers
2013 Opera North Children's Chorus
2013 Park Lane Group – young artists

## ■ School music projects: applications followed by interviews

1997 'Music-Making for All' – teaching project, Coventry
1997 'New Curwen Method, and forming pilot group' – Burnham-on-Crouch, Essex
1998 'Create an Original Opera' – Bebington, Wirral
1998 'Cross-Curricular Effects of Stage Productions in Primary Schools' – Amersham, Bucks.
1998 'The Development of Children's Compositional Skills at Key Stage 2' – Herstmonceux, East Sussex
1999 'New Era – New Generation – New Composition' – Key Stages 3, 4 & 5, Macclesfield, Cheshire
2002 'Introducing Indonesian Gamelan into Argyll Primary School' – Walthamstow, London

2002  'Stamping, Clapping and Chanting in Relation to Cognitive Functions in School Children' – Bedford

2002  'Voices in Concert: Peripatetic Instrumental and Vocal Teachers' – Slough, Berks.

2003  'Beginning Violin Group: Peer Mentoring Project' – Birmingham

2003  Establishing a county schools singing group – Northumberland

2003  Running Addington Voices Youth Choir – Croydon

2005  'Music Games: The Easy Way to Learn Theory' – Cheshire

2005  'Quartets for Kids' – Lincolnshire

2005  'The Dub-Dub-Dub Player Experience' – internet composition, Northwich, Cheshire.

2005  'The Newtons Colour Strings Project' – Romford, Essex

2006  Production of Method: 'A Starter for Ten'

2007  School opera project – Honiton, Devon

2010  'Magical Music Box' project – Hertingfordbury Cooper Primary School, Herts

# Index